THE LANGUAGE OF POETRY

THE LANGUAGE
OF POETRY

BY

Philip Wheelwright · Cleanth Brooks
I. A. Richards · Wallace Stevens

Edited by Allen Tate

New York
RUSSELL & RUSSELL
1960

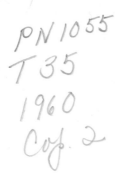

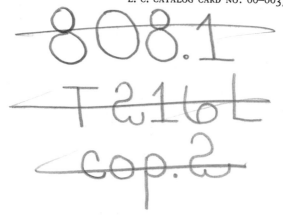

PRINTED IN THE UNITED STATES OF AMERICA

PREFACE

*T*HE four essays collected here under the title *The Language of Poetry* were read to audiences at Princeton University in the spring of 1941 under the auspices of the Creative Arts Program. The primary aim of the symposium was not a series of lectures but the present book. The contributors were invited to prepare essays which should not sacrifice the difficult implications of the subject to the limited capacity of the ear of even the best audience.

"Semantics" is the term popularly given at present to the subject of this book; yet semantics is the study of the relevance of terms and statements to objects and events, and is thus only one of the problems of the language of poetry. We are witnessing in America today an exhaustive study of poetic language such as criticism has not attempted either here or in Europe in any previous age. Whether this means that we shall get better poetry or better criticism, or both, it is too soon to know; if we find after a generation that we have got neither, it will be too late to do anything about it. At present we may see a shift, in talking about poetry, from psychology to philosophy—from poetry as emotion and response to poetry as a kind of knowledge.

It is always proper to ask Mr. Richards to join a critical symposium; we asked him on this occasion because we may observe in his own intellectual history the shift that I refer to; and we wished to acknowledge him as the pioneer of our age in this field of study. The symposium comes to a unanimous decision on one question, but it is the main question: that poetry, although it is not science, is not nonsense. It is a modest conclusion, but one which, in the recent state of criticism, could not be assumed or even easily arrived at.

The Creative Arts Program is grateful to the contributors for their cooperation, and to the Mesures Fund for bringing them to Princeton. This Fund, which has been given to the Creative Arts Program by the editor of *Mesures,* the French quarterly now temporarily suspended, provides for four more symposiums on literary problems. To Mr. Henry Church, the donor, we owe our chief gratitude.

ALLEN TATE

CONTENTS

POETRY · MYTH · AND REALITY

BY PHILIP WHEELWRIGHT

POETRY · MYTH · AND REALITY

PHILIP WHEELWRIGHT

*P*OETRY suffers today from at once too high and too low an appraisal. We burden Shakespeare with flatteries which his contemporaries would have reserved for royalty or for the ancients, but there is reason to believe that modern theater audiences are insensitive to much in his plays that the rowdier but more perceptive frequenters of the Globe Theater took in as an expected part of the entertainment. Charged language, language of associative complexity, is a rarity on the stage or in the cinema today, and when it occurs it is likely to embarrass by its artiness, its rather too evident snob appeal. We read poetry as a special discipline, becoming scholarly about it or ecstatic about it according to our profession, temperament and mood, but we deprecate its intrusion into the sober business of everyday living. Poetry seems to most of us something to be set upon a pedestal and left there, like one of those chaste heroines of medieval romance, high and dry.

Why is there this impoverishment of response toward poetry in present-day society? The question may be one of the most important we can ask, for it concerns not poetry and poetic response alone, but by implication the general sickness of our contemporary world. The symptoms, though diverse, are connected; and I suspect we shall not understand why great poetry is no longer written in an age which endows innumerable lecturers to talk about poetry, unless we also understand why it is that we must let our fellow-countrymen starve in an era of productive plenty, and why as Americans we spent twenty years professing our love of peace and democracy while helping to finance dictatorships and throttle democracies on three continents, and why as Christians we think it proper to build imposing churches while treating God as something out of last year's Sunday supplement. The question of poetry's status in the present-day world is interrelated with such questions as these, and it seems to me that we cannot adequately understand any one of the questions except in a perspective that catches at least the outlines of the others. The needed perspective is to my mind a mytho-religious one, without any of the claptrap sometimes associated with either word; for it involves a rediscovery of the original and essentially unchangeable conditions of human insight and human blessedness. The aim of this lecture is to indicate the nature of that perspective and to discover its latent presence in some of the great poetry of past times.

Suppose we represent the dimensions of human experience, very tentatively, by means of a diagram,— where the horizontal line E-P represents the dimension of secular experience, *empirical* experience as I think we may call it without redundancy; of that trafficking with things, relations and ideas that makes up our everyday commonsense world. It has two poles: outwardly there are the phenomena (P) that constitute our physical universe; these are space-

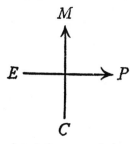

like, are interrelated by causal laws, and are the proper object of scientific inquiry. At the other pole of this horizontal axis stands the ego (E) which knows the phenomena—partly as a spectator and partly no doubt as a contributor to their connection and significance. The major philosophical movements of the past three centuries owe their character and their limitations to the stress, I think the undue stress, which they have put upon the horizontal axis. Descartes made the additional mistake of hypostatizing E and P, establishing the thinking self and the extended world of things over against each other as distinct substances; he "cut the universe in two with a hatchet," as Hegel said, separating it into two absolutely alien spheres, thought without extension and extension without thought: thereby settling the direction, perhaps the doom, of modern philosophy. Granted that the Cartesian bifurcation was immensely fruitful for the subsequent development of natural science, the benefit was purely one of conceptual efficiency, not of interpretive fulness. The general result was to alienate nature from man by denuding it of human significance, and thereby deprive man of his natural sense of continuity with the environing world, leaving him to face the Absolute alone. To this stark confrontation the Cartesian man brings a single talisman—pure reason, which, rightly used, can answer all questions, solve all mysteries, illumine every dark cranny in the universal scheme. All truth becomes to the unobstructed reason as clear and indubitable as the truth of an arithmetical sum. A child who performs an arithmetical sum correctly—so Descartes declares—knows the utmost, with respect to that sum, that the human mind, and by implication God's mind, can ever discover. Analogously a physicist, by confining himself to clear and distinct ideas, may come to know the utmost, with respect to any given problem, that can possibly be known; and this would be true, on Cartesian principles, even of a psychologist or a theologian or a student of any field whatever who adhered to properly rational methods. Athene springs full-born from the head of Zeus; or to use a more modern simile, wisdom consists in a sort of klieg-light brilliance rather than in adjusting one's eyes to the chiaroscuro of the familiar world. For the familiar world—here is its essential defect to a rationalist like Descartes—has a past, it develops, is time-burdened, and draws much of its

meaning from shared tradition; while to Descartes'
view tradition, except so far as reason can justify it,
is superstition, loyalties to the past are servile, and
the philosopher should be like an architect who tears
down the lovable old houses and crooked streets of a
medieval town in order to erect a symmetrical city
where no one can lose his way. Thus in this rational-
istic philosophy of Descartes we have, close to its
modern source, the deadliest of all heresies. It is the
sin, or, if you prefer, the delusion, of intellectual
pride, a reenactment of Adam's fall and of the building of Bab-el, and it leads in our time to the fallacy of
hoping for a future without organically remembering
a past, the imbecility of trying to build history out
of an unhistorical present.

The influence of Descartes' dualistic rationalism
has been far-flung. In subsequent philosophy, although various parts of his doctrine became modified
or rejected, the Cartesian way of conceiving human
experience, as an individual ego able by its own
powers to know the world of phenomena confronting it, played a decisive rôle. British empiricists and
positivists in particular, from Locke through Hume
and Mill right down to Bertrand Russell and a ma-
jority of professional philosophers in our own day,
have differed from one another not in any doubt as
to the self-sufficiency of the horizontal axis of experience but in their particular ways of distinguishing
or connecting or distributing the emphasis between
the ego and its objects. Today the horizontal philos-

ophy has reached its clearest and most intractable expression in the related doctrines of behaviorism, instrumentalism, and semantic positivism: behaviorism, which reduces the human mind to what can be experimentally observed of its bodily behavior; instrumentalism, which reduces the meaning of any concept to that set of experimental operations by which the denotation of the concept could be objectively shown; and semantic positivism, which aims at a one-to-one correspondence between units of language and the sets or types of objects and events which such language-units denote. These three doctrines, which may be grouped under the general name of positivistic materialism, have acquired great prestige in our time. Every honest and sane intellectual must, I believe, come to grips with them: must recognize both that they are the logically inescapable outcome and expression of our secular way of life, and that they are utterly disastrous. The only truth on this basis is experimental truth, structures built out of the common denominators of human experience; religious truth and poetic truth are dismissed as fictions, as misnomers. Religion ceases to have more than a tentative and subjective validity: it expresses the yearnings and fears and awe-struck impotence of human minds with respect to events and sequences in the external world which up to a given stage of human development have eluded scientific explanation and experimental control. Poetry, likewise, has no truth-value that is distinctive to it as poetry. It contains, on the one hand, a "subject" (in Matthew Arnold's sense), a "scenario," a literal meaning, which could be expressed without essential loss in the language of science; and beyond this there is only the pleasurable decoration and emotional heightening which the form and evocative language of the poem bestows. The poet is not in any sense a seer or a prophet; he is simply, in the jargon of advertising, an effective layout man. Science has thus become the Great Dictator, to whom the spiritual republics of religion and poetry are yielding up their autonomy in bloodless defeat. There is no help for it within the purely horizontal perspective of human experience: if we see the world only as patterns of phenomena, our wisdom will be confined to such truths as phenomena can furnish. And this situation is very barren and very unpromising, not only for religion and for poetry, but for expanding love and the sense of *radical significance* which are at the root of both.

Now my belief is that the problem as posited exclusively in terms of the horizontal consciousness is an unnatural problem, an intellectual monstrosity which leads away from, rather than toward, the greater and more enduring truths. No genuine religious teacher, and with the lone exception of Lucretius no great poet, has ever sought truth in exclusively empirical terms; and I must say I find deeper truths, richer and more relevant truths, in the mysticism of Lao-tse and Jesus, in the dramatic suggestiveness of Aeschylus and Shakespeare, than in the impersonal experiments of scientists or the voluminous literalism of scholars. How then are we to validate, and in what terms are we to discuss, the transempirical factor in truth which is presupposed in all religion and in all the profounder sort of poetry?

The thing required of us, I believe, if we are to escape the blind alley of empirical positivism, is a proper understanding of myth, and of mythical consciousness. It is the habit of secular thought to dismiss myth either as pure fiction, a set of fairy-tales with which the human race in childhood frittered away its time; or else as allegory—that is, as a round-about and inexact way of expressing truths about physical and human nature which could be expressed just as pertinently and much more accurately by the language of science. On either interpretation myth becomes regarded as an archaism, a barren survival, with no function of its own which cannot be served more efficiently by more up-to-date language and methods; a kind of fiction that should be renounced as completely as possible by the serious truth-seeker. What I want to stress is that this secular, positivistic attitude toward myth appears to me quite inadequate to explain the facts—I mean, of course, the salient, the really interesting aspect of the facts. It ignores or deprecates that haunting awareness of transcendental forces peering through the cracks of the visible universe, that is the very essence of myth. It blandly overlooks the possibility, which to Aeschylus, Dante,

Shakespeare and many others was an axiom of assured faith, that myth may have a non-exchangeable semantic function of its own—that myth may express visions of truth to which the procedures of the scientist are grossly irrelevant; that the mythical consciousness, in short, (to exploit a convenient mathematical metaphor) may be a dimension of experience cutting across the empirical dimension as an independent variable.

In the foregoing diagram I have represented the mythico-religious dimension of human experience by a vertical line C-M cutting across the horizontal axis E-P.

C represents the community mind, which is to myth more or less what the individual mind is to science; and the upper pole M represents Mystery, of which the community mind is darkly aware. Thus the semantic arrow points from C to M, as it points from E to P. This double relation should not be conceived too rigidly: scientific truth is admittedly established by some degree of social cooperation, and mythical truth is apprehended and given form by individuals. Nevertheless the distinction is basically sound. Myth is the expression of a profound sense of togetherness—a togetherness not merely upon the plane of intellect, as is primarily the case among fellow-scientists, but a togetherness of feeling and of action and of wholeness of living. Such togetherness must have, moreover, a history. Community mind is nothing so sporadic as the mass mind of a modern lynching party or a wave of war hysteria, nor even is it found to any considerable degree in a trade union. In such manifestations as these the collective mind possesses little or no significant pattern, for it has had no time to mature. It creates not myths but merely ideologies—an ideology being a sort of parvenu myth which expresses not the interests of the group as a cooperative organism but the interests of each member of the group reflected and repeated in each other member: to this extent it lacks also a transcendental reference. A mass cannot create myths, for it has had no real history. Myths are the expression of a community mind which has enjoyed long natural growth, so that the sense of togetherness becomes patterned and semantically significant. A patterned sense of togetherness develops its proper rhythms in ceremony and prayer, dance and song; and just as the micro-rhythms of the eye project themselves as a visible world of trees and stones, and as the micro-rhythms of the ear project themselves as an audible world of outer sounds, so the larger rhythms of community life project themselves as a sense of enveloping Mystery. In cultures where the mythico-religious consciousness has developed freely, this sense of mystery tinges all cognition: whether called *mana* as by the Melanesians, or *wakonda* as by the Sioux Indians, or *brahma* as by the early Aryan invaders of India, there is felt to be a mysterious Other, a spirit or breath in the world, which is more real, more awful, and in the higher religions

more reverenceable than the visible and obvious par-
ticulars of experience, while at the same time it may
manifest or embody itself in persons, things, words
and acts in unforeseeable ways. Sometimes this basic
Mystery becomes dispersed and personified into a
polytheism of gods and daemons, sometimes concentrated and exalted into a single majestic God. Whatever its eventual form, it appears to express on the
one hand man's primordial way of knowing, before
the individual has separated himself with clear critical
awareness from the group; and on the other hand
an indispensable element in the cognitive activity
of every vital culture, primitive or civilized. What
I am arguing, in short, is not merely that the consciousness which arises from group-life and group-
memories is the original matrix of individual consciousness—that much is a sociological truism—but
that when the consciousness of individuals separates
itself too utterly from the sustaining warmth of the
common myth-consciousness, the dissociated consciousness becomes in time unoriented and sterile,
fit for neither great poetry nor great wisdom nor
great deeds.

What concerns the student of poetry most directly
is the relation of myth to speech, the characteristic
forms in which the mythical consciousness finds utterance. Shelley declared truly that "in the infancy
of society every author is a poet, because language
itself is poetry"; and, we may add, the reason why
primitive language is poetry lies in the fact that it

is the spontaneous expression of a consciousness so largely, in our sense, mythical. There are two outstanding respects in which primitive language, and especially spoken language, tends to be poetic, or at any rate to have a natural kinship with poetry: first, in its manner of utterance, its rhythms and euphonies; second, in its manner of reference, in the delicacy and associative fulness with which it refers to various aspects of the all-encompassing Mystery. In short, primitive speech—for I am dealing here with language that is meant to be spoken—employs both rhythm and metaphor. The reasons for the possession of these characteristics by primitive speech are doubtless clear from the foregoing description of the mythical consciousness. Primitive speech is a more direct expression of the community mind than speech that has grown sophisticated, and rhythm is the vehicle by which the sense of community is projected and carried through time. Rhythm has furthermore a magical function: for since the primitive community mind is not limited to a society of actual living persons but embraces also the ghosts of ancestors and the souls of things in the environing world, the rhythms of gesture and speech are felt to include and to exert a binding effect not only upon men but, when conducted under auspicious conditions, upon ghosts, gods, and nature; which is the essence of magic. Such language thus possesses a naturally evocative quality: it is felt as having a tendency to endow the world with the qualities which it declares to be there. The metaphorical character of primitive language, on the other hand, consists in its tendency to be rather manifoldly allusive: it can be so, because of the varied associations with which communication within a closed society has gradually become charged; and it has a semantic necessity of being so, because only in language having multiple reference can the full, manifold, and paradoxical character of the primordial Mystery find fit expression. Owing to such referential plenitude the language of primitives tends to employ paradox freely: it makes use of statements contradicting each other and of statements contradicting an experientially accepted situation; for the Mystery which it tries to express cannot be narrowed down to logical categories.

The island of Fiji furnishes a particularly interesting illustration of uses to which primitive poetry can be put. When a Fijian dies, the legend is that his ghost spends three days traversing the fifty-mile path that leads from the principal Fijian city to the sacred mountain Naukavadra, situated on the western coast of the isle. This mountain has a ledge overlooking the sea, called Nai-thombo-thombo, "the jumping-off place," from which the departing ghost hurls itself down and swims to a distant paradise beyond the sunset, where it rejoins its ancestors. Before the final immersion, however, the ghost on arriving at the sacred mountain is received hospitably in a cave

by the ghosts of ancient hero-ancestors, guardians
of the tribe's morality and well-being. After a feast,
partly cannibal, has been eaten in common and ancient
tribal lays have been sung, the newcomer finds his
spiritual eyes awakened, and realizing for the first
time that death has befallen him he is overwhelmed
with grief. To the accompaniment of native instruments, addressing the ancestors he chants these
words:

My Lords! In evil fashion are we buried,
Buried staring up into heaven,
We see the scud flying over the sky,
We are worn out with the feet tramping on us.

Our ribs, the rafters of our house, are torn asunder,
The eyes with which we gazed on one another are
    destroyed,
The nose with which we kissed has fallen in,
The breast with which we embraced is ruined,
The mouth with which we laughed at one another
    has decayed,
The teeth with which we bit have showered down.
Gone is the hand that threw the tinka stick.
The testes have rolled away.

Hark to the lament of the mosquito!
It is well that *he* should die and pass onward.
But alas for my ear that he has devoured.

Hark to the lament of the fly!
It is well that *he* should die and pass onward.
But alas! he has stolen the eye from which I drank.

Hark to the lament of the black ant!
It is well that *he* should die and pass onward.
But alas for my whale's-tooth* that he has devoured.

The dead man's meeting with the ancestors takes place on the third day after death, and is followed by the leap into the sea and the passage over into the afterworld. Thus far we are in the realm of myth. Parallel to the myth-pattern is a behavior-pattern which is traditional with the survivors. On the third day they bury the now putrefying corpse, and while doing so they chant ceremonially the same songs that the dead man hears and sings in the cave at Mt. Naukavadra. Evidently the cause-effect relation involved is complex. Sociological analysis will regard the belief as a fictional projection which has the function of explaining and justifying the tribal burial processes; while to the survivors, on the other hand, the matter appears in reverse, their ceremonies being designed to annotate, and by imitative magic to assist, the dead one's situation. In any case the dirge I have just quoted serves by its strongly marked rhythms, inescapable even in translation, to establish a sense of widened community, whereby, for the duration of the ceremony at least, the chanting survivors, the recently deceased, and the ancient ancestor-gods are brought into a strongly felt and tersely articulated togetherness. Such expressions of a widened community-sense, paced in the tribal calendar according

* Whale's-tooth: the phallus; also used (in its literal sense) as a symbol of wealth and medium of exchange.

to the occurrence of emotionally significant events like births and deaths, puberty, marriage, and war, are the most vitalizing forces in tribal cultural life.

In ancient Egypt a similar phenomenon was current, although in Egyptian death chants the magical element is more explicit. The Pyramid Texts—those ancient inscriptions dating from the fourth millennium B.C. which are found on the inner walls of the pyramid tombs—are records of the royal chants by which bands of faithful subjects, led ceremonially by the high priests, helped the Pharaoh whom they were burying there to secure immortal divinity. Here, in part, is one of the noblest of these texts:

> The flier flies from earth to sky.
> Upward he soars like a heron,
> Upward he leaps like a grasshopper,
> Kissing the sky like a hawk.
>
> Crowned with the headdress of the sun god,
> Wearing the hawk's plumage,
> Upward he flies to join his brothers the gods.
> Joyously we behold him.
>
> Now we give back your heart, Osiris.
> Now we give back your feet, Osiris.
> Now we give back your arms, Osiris.
>
> Flying aloft like a bird,
> He settles down like a beetle
> On a seat in the ship of the sun-god.
> Now he rows your ship across the sky, O Glowing
>   One!

Now he brings your ship to land, O Glowing One!
And when again you ascend out of the horizon,
He will be there with staff in hand,
The navigator of your ship, O Glowing One!

The primordial gods, the ancient nine, are dazzled,
The Lords of Forms are shaken with terror
As he breaks the metallic sky asunder.
Older than the Great One, he issues commands.
Eternity is set before him,
Discernment is placed at his feet,
The horizon is given to his keeping.

The sky is darkened, the stars rain down,
The bones of the earth-god tremble
When this one steps forth as a god
Devouring his fathers and mothers,
With the sacred serpents on his forehead.

Men and gods he devours.
His sky-dwelling servants prepare the cooking-pots,
Wiping them out with the legs of their women.
The gods are cooked for him piece by piece
In the cooking-pots of the sky at evening.

Cracking the backbones he eats the spinal marrow,
He swallows the hearts and lungs of the Wise Ones.
Their wisdom and their strength has passed into his
    belly.
Their godhood is within him.

The community-sense expressed in this hymn has
a definite but again complex pattern. On the plane of
earthly actuality the celebrants feel their union in a
shared joy at the heavenly prowess of their dead

king. On the transcendental plane, the plane of myth, there is another sort of union—an identification of the dead king with Osiris, god of periodic and perpetual rebirth, and with Ra the sun god. Although a reverent distinction is observed between the worshippers and the "Osirified One," the exalted king-god whose deification they celebrate, nevertheless the surviving community enjoys a vicarious participation in godhood, since the Pharaoh is felt to be still the worshippers' representative and the symbol of their communal solidarity as he had been on earth. That sense of mystical community, in Egypt as elsewhere, found its natural expression in a type of poetry characterized by marked rhythms and transcendental imagery, which are the esthetic correlates of the lower and upper poles of myth-consciousness.

Thus the logic of myth proceeds on different assumptions from the logic of science and of secular realism, and moves by different laws. Attempts to deal with myth by the methods of science fall inevitably short of the mark. While objective methods of inquiry can trace the occasions of myth, the conditions under which it may flourish, they are quite incapable of understanding the mythical consciousness itself. For science and myth are basically incommensurate ways of experiencing, and science cannot "explain" myth without explaining it away. Its explanations are not interpretive but pragmatically reductive. The questions which science poses about myth are never quite relevant, for the questions essential to myth are patterned on a different syntax. Always in scientific thinking there is the implicit assumption of an "either-or" situation. Is the Pharaoh identical with Osiris after death or is he not? If so, and if all the Pharaohs who ruled before him share the identity, it follows (by the logic of science) that they must be identical with each other; and in that case why are they buried and worshipped individually? Moreover, if identification with Osiris is the soul's final attainment, as the Pyramid Texts indicate, why is the corpse mummified as if to preserve symbolically, and perhaps magically, just this individual to whom the body had once belonged? Such questions as these do not admit of any logically clear answer, and it is important for the understanding both of myth and of poetry to see why they do not. Science seeks clarity of an outward, publicly recognizable kind; it can regard mysteries as but materials for its particular techniques of clarification. By scientific logic a thing is either A or B and not both; or, if both, its double character must mean either that the thing is complex and can be dissociated into A and B as its elements, or else that A and B share a common quality K which with sufficient care is susceptible of exact description. The tendency of science is always to think in terms of mechanical models—structures analyzable into parts which, added up, remake the originals. Mechanical operations do work in that way, but wholeness of experience does not, and myth is an expression of whole experiences that whole men have known and felt.

Passing from primitive poetry to the poetry of more civilized eras, we find that while a greater proportion of the poem is contributed by the genius of some individual poet, yet in those poems which carry the signature of greatness, myth still plays a prominent and usually a more deliberate rôle. Myth is invaluable to the poet, furnishing as it does a background of familiar reference by which the sensibilities of the poet and his readers are oriented and so brought into profounder communication than would otherwise have been possible. The ways in which myth is poetically employed, and the effects gained by its employment, depend not only upon the artistry of the individual poet but also upon the general attitude toward myth in the age in which he has the good or bad luck to be born. He may be born, like Aeschylus or Dante, in a period when a substantial body of myths enjoys wide acceptance as literally true: his greatest poems in such case will be poetic intensifications and elaborations of some of those myths. He may be born, like Virgil or Shakespeare, at a time when a more sophisticated attitude toward myths is beginning to set in but before it has made such headway as to drain the myths of all vitality: the poet will then employ his myths thematically, breaking them up and redistributing their elements as may best suit his esthetic purpose. Or he may be born, finally, in an age like our own, in the late afternoon of a culture, when the myths that once moved men to great deeds now survive as antiquarian curiosities: such a poet will feel himself to be living in a cultural wasteland, his materials will be fragmentary and un-promising, and while he may prove an ingenious renovator of ruined monuments or a resourceful prac-titioner of metajournalism, his contribution as a poet ––the contribution of a whole man who speaks pow-erfully to whole men—will be small.

Aeschylus, the first great dramatic poet of the West, exemplifies the early condition of civilized poetry in its relation to myth. In his time the chorus of dancing priests, which probably stemmed from ancient religious rituals associated with Dionysus and the grain-goddess Demeter, had become partly secularized, until, although the religious background was still a vital part of the whole show and amply familiar to the playgoing Greeks, the predominant purpose of the great dramatic festivals had insensibly slipped from worship to entertainment. The specta-tors, who in an earlier age had no doubt participated in the ritualistic dance, were now become relatively immunized: their function is to sit still and at proper times to applaud and perhaps even to chant in unison some of the choric refrains—a practice apparently indicated by the closing exhortation of *The Eumen-ides*. But atavistically they are still religious cele-brants, being led in their observances by the band of rhythmically chanting priests, which has now become the tragic chorus; their emotions pulsate synchronically with those which the chorus expresses by word and gesture, and their acceptance of the dramatic situations which unfold themselves is largely governed by this dramatic communion.

The characteristic problem of Aeschylean drama is human guilt and its consequences. In the Greek mind two conceptions of destiny and of guilt interplayed: the Olympian and the chthonic. According to the former conception man's cardinal guilt was *hybris,* pride, which consisted in trying to overstep the boundary that separated man's ordained lot from that of the blessed and deathless gods, while virtue consisted in observing due measure, remaining loyal to one's destined station in life, and especially to one's condition of earthbound mortal manhood. The Olympian conception was thus at bottom *spacelike,* a matter of observing boundaries, limits and middle paths: indeed, in Hesiod's *Works and Days* it is particularized, in what may have been its original form, as an admonition to till one's own soil and not trespass on one's neighbor's. The chthonic conception, on the other hand, related guilt to the earth (*chthôn*), which became infectiously polluted when innocent blood was spilled, and to the vengeful ancestor ghosts who, living within the earth, were offended by actions that weakened the power and prestige, or violated the moral code, of the tribe or nation to which they still in a manner belonged. Thus the ghost of King Darius, in *The Persians,* returns from the underworld to berate his royal son for leading the Persian

host into a disastrous war; and thus too the three
Furies (originally snakes and still wearing snaky
locks at the beginning of *The Eumenides*) haunt
Orestes for his crime of matricide; and thus again
in Sophocles' *Oedipus Rex* a plague has fallen on the
land and cannot be removed until the unwitting mur-
der and incest have been brought to light and ex-
piated. In all these cases the dominant motif is the
rhythmic succession of guilt and expiation, which at
once expresses the ingrained Greek sense of a rhythmically pulsating nature in which moral qualities like
physical ones undergo seasonal alteration, while at
the same time it provides a forceful and intelligible
form into which tragic drama can be moulded. There
is a clear sense, therefore, in which the chthonic conception of guilt tends to be *timelike,* a matter of
working out the patterned destiny of an individual
or family or city or nation.

Clearly the chthonic conception of destiny lends
itself to representation most readily through the
time-charged medium of tragic drama, the Olympian
conception through the relatively static medium of
the epic. The distinction is a shifting one, however: in
the sculpturally conceived *Prometheus Bound* the
Olympian conception appears to predominate, while
in that one great surviving trilogy, the *Oresteia,* the
chthonic theme of guilt and retribution is intertwined
with Olympian imagery, until in the end both elements
are sublimated in a magnificent patriotic finale, by
which the dramatic community-sense is explicitly

secularized. Nevertheless it is worth noting that in the *Oresteia,* which without much dispute may stand as his greatest work, Aeschylus is more respectful and attaches greater dramatic and moral importance to chthonic than to Olympian ideas. He dismisses gravely the Olympian myth that the gods envy human prosperity, while the chthonic myth of the inheritance of guilt haunts him right through to the end, and motivates the long tortured struggle that constitutes the three dramas. Again, in the final play of the trilogy, although Apollo is strangely ridiculed, the Furies are treated with exaggerated respect, as powers who must be placated and even reverenced since they are the life-germ of Athenian moral and political life. All in all, the time-myth, as Nietzsche's *The Birth of Tragedy* explosively demonstrates, is at the core of Greek as of every other vital culture, and when its rhythms become weakened or vulgarized the culture grows senile.

Magic, which has played so large and so explicit a rôle in primitive poetry, appears in Aeschylean drama in sublimated form. For what is magic but operation through a direct emotional congruence established between the operator and his object? The dramatist no longer operates like the primitive magician upon gods and daemons and unnamed mysterious forces of the outer world. His magic is turned, at least to a very large degree, upon the responsive feelings of his audience. We still speak today of a dramatist's "magic," but the compliment is usually vapid. In Greek tragedy the word was applicable more literally, as through the medium of rhythmic chants with musical and choreographic accompaniment, behind which lay the common heritage of mythological background that found stylized expression in plot and imagery, the vast throng that packed the City Dionysia was brought for a few hours into significant emotional unity. Aristotle has noted the katharsis of pity and terror which takes place on such occasions, but they do not exhaust the emotional effect. Deeper than they and deeper than any conscious recognition is the communally felt, ceremonially induced emotion of religious awe, by which the Greek spectators in a miraculous bubble of time are caught up and momentarily identified with the transcendental forces that envelop them and impregnate their culture.

Shakespeare was of course a more eclectic mythologer. As a master-dramatist he could adapt expertly to poetic and dramatic uses the myths that colored the popular consciousness of his time. And yet there is in Shakespeare's mythical consciousness a deep-lying unity, which becomes gradually visible as we trace in their varied expressions what I suggest are the two Shakespearean key-myths—the myth of love and the myth of divine and earthly governance. Every play that Shakespeare wrote shows a large concern with one or the other and usually both of these themes— if not in plot, at least in imagery and allusion.

The love myth enjoys a varied and imagistically colored career in its earlier expressions—*Venus and*

Adonis, the Sonnets, such comedies as *Love's Labour's Lost,* and culminating in *Romeo and Juliet.*
Love, as represented here, although often strikingly
realistic—

> He wrings her nose, he strikes her on the cheeks,
> He bends her fingers, holds her pulses hard, . . .

is much more than a transient phenomenon of human
experience. Unlike the anarchy of lust, love is a harmony, a sweet concord, a transcendently heard music;
and Venus' consuming passion for Adonis strikes
the reader as sufficiently redeemed and justified by its
harmonization with the universal passion that throbs
through nature. Venus' desire, allied by pedigree
with the high concerns of the gods, becomes merged
in the poem with such natural manifestations as the
strong-necked stallion who breaks rein on espying a
young breeding mare:

> Imperiously he leaps, he neighs, he bounds,
> And now his woven girths he breaks asunder;
> The bearing earth with his hard hoof he wounds,
> Whose hollow womb resounds like heaven's thunder;
>   The iron bit he crusheth 'tween his teeth,
>   Controlling what he was controlled with.
>
> His ears up-prick'd; his braided hanging mane
> Upon his compass'd crest now stand on end;
> His nostrils drink the air, and forth again,
> As from a furnace, vapors doth he send;
>   His eye, which scornfully glisters like fire,
>   Shows his hot courage and his high desire.

The sexual and procreative imagery of these stanzas needs no underlining. But the important thing is that love and procreation are joined—here by imagery as later, in the Sonnets, by explicit statement:

> And nothing 'gainst Time's scythe can make defence
> Save breed, to brave him when he takes thee hence.

This couplet introduces the villain of the love-myth: Time, who devours like a cormorant all of this present breath's endeavors. Or rather, all save one. For through the medium of art man can rise above his mortal existence, and making himself the heir of all eternity can bate the scythe's keen edge.

> Yet do thy worst, old Time; despite thy wrong,
> My love shall in my verse ever live young.

Poetry and music uphold the immortality of love in all Shakespeare's plays; love's frailty or perversion is announced by jangling discordant rhythms, with the frequent imagistic accompaniment of tempests as indicative of discord in nature.

The myth of universal governance, divine and earthly, has its double source in Christianity and in Elizabethan patriotic consciousness; like the love-myth it expresses a harmony that joins mankind with divinty and with ordered nature.

> The heavens themselves, the planets, and this center
> Observe degree, priority, and place.
>   . . . But when the planets
> In evil mixture to disorder wander,
> What plagues and what portents! what mutiny!

> What raging of the sea! shaking of earth!
> Commotion in the winds! Frights, changes, horrors,
> Divert and crack, rend and deracinate
> The unity and married calm of states
> Quite from their fixture.

These plagues and portents, tempests and deracinations, symbolize the inverse side of the governance-myth: they accompany—at first in verbal imagery, then later in actual stage-presentation—not only the regicide of a Caesar and a Duncan, but the insurrections of man's inner state which are always the most crucial motivation of Shakespearean tragedy. The myth of governance affirms "degree, priority and place" at once in the political order, in nature, in the soul of man, and in the divine government of the world; now one, now another of these aspects is given foremost emphasis, and at times the last of them is denied, according to the contextual requirements of the individual drama. But in the king-god imagery of *Richard II,* in the allegorical overtones of *Measure for Measure* and *The Tempest,* in the demonology of *Macbeth,* and most subtly of all in the tragic katharsis of *King Lear,* the unity is reaffirmed: earthly and divine government, the order of nature, and the nobility of man are brought again and again into symbolic and always somewhat incomplete identification.

Running through and giving form to the other mythical material, there is, in the greater achievements of Shakespeare, the myth of tragedy itself. This myth, which attains increasingly full realization in Shakespeare's successive experiments with tragedy up to and including *Lear,* finally receives brief explicit utterance in Edmund's cry:

The wheel is come full circle; I am here.

We today have lost this sense of cyclical fulness and therewith of transcendental significance in human affairs; accordingly we no longer produce great tragedy, because we no longer believe in the tragic myth. In its place we have substituted the shabbier myth of comedy, which Shakespeare utilized for a time and then, when it had lost its power to move him dramatically, unleashed his contempt by expressing it as the title of one of his worst and weakest plays, "All's Well That Ends Well." This wretched quarter-truth is exploited in most of the novels and nearly all of the movies of our day—no longer as healthy comedy merely, but decked out with false sentimentality in the trappings that once belonged to tragedy. Our failure in tragic intuition, our substitution for it of bathos and business practicality in loose-wedded conjunction, is not least among the disastrous factors of the contemporary world.

These considerations of the rôle of myth in great poetry of the past may throw some light upon the predicament of the poet and the unpromising estate of poetry in our non-mythological present. The poet of today—and by that I mean the poetic impetus in all of us today—is profoundly inhibited by the dearth

of shared consciousness of myth. Our current moti-
vating ideas are not myths but ideologies, lacking transcendental significance. This loss of myth-consciousness I believe to be the most devastating loss that
humanity can suffer; for as I have argued, myth-
consciousness is the bond that unites men both with
one another and with the unplumbed Mystery from
which mankind is sprung and without reference to
which the radical significance of things goes to pot.
Now a world bereft of radical significance is not long
tolerated; it leaves men radically unstable, so that
they will seize at any myth or pseudo-myth that is
offered. There have been ages of scepticism in the
past, and they have always succumbed in time to new
periods of belief, sometimes of violent fanaticism. It
appears to me historically probable that whether we
like it or not, our own present philosophy of liberal
democratic scepticism will be succeeded within the
next generation, perhaps sooner, by a recrudescence of
myth-consciousness in America, although we can
only dimly foresee what form that consciousness will
take. Probably it will include a strong consciousness
of America and the American destiny, but the important question is whether it will include something
more—whether America will become a genuine symbol or merely a dogma. The myth of the nation must
be shot through with a larger, transcendent mythological consciousness, or it lacks sanctity and in the
long run will not satisfy the deeper human cravings.
But we have to reckon with the possibility that this

development will not take place at once. History does serve human needs, but not on the table d'hote plan; the preparations are slow and we have to expect a certain amount of bungling in the kitchen. Perhaps our immediate prospect is one of darkness, and waiting, and wholesale liquidation of much that has seemed indispensable to us, spiritual as well as material. We do not know what is to come; we can only try to learn what we must do. I suspect we must be like starving men who keep a little from their meager store to plant it in the ground for a future crop. The poetry of our time doesn't matter much, it is a last echo of something important that was alive long ago. What matters is the myth-consciousness of the next generations, the spiritual seed that we plant in our children; their loves and insights and incubating sense of significant community. On that depend the possibilities of future greatness—in poetry and in everything else.

THE LANGUAGE OF PARADOX

BY CLEANTH BROOKS

THE LANGUAGE OF PARADOX

CLEANTH BROOKS

*F*EW OF US are prepared to accept the statement
that the language of poetry is the language of paradox. Paradox is the language of sophistry, hard,
bright, witty; it is hardly the language of the soul.
We are willing to allow that paradox is a permissible
weapon which a Chesterton may on occasion exploit.
We may permit it in epigram, a special subvariety of
poetry; and in satire, which though useful, we are
hardly willing to allow to be poetry at all. Our preju-
dices force us to regard paradox as intellectual rather
than emotional, clever rather than profound, rational
rather than divinely irrational.

Yet there is a sense in which paradox is the language appropriate and inevitable to poetry. It is the
scientist whose truth requires a language purged of
every trace of paradox; apparently the truth which the
poet utters can be approached only in terms of paradox. I overstate the case, to be sure; it is possible that
the title of this paper is itself to be treated as merely a
paradox. Certainly, the paper itself will appear to
many people as merely a piece of special case-making,
specious rather than convincing. But there are reasons
for thinking that the overstatement which I propose

may light up some elements in the nature of poetry which tend to be overlooked.

The case of William Wordsworth, for instance, is instructive on this point. His poetry would not appear to promise many examples of the language of paradox. He usually prefers the direct attack. He insists on simplicity; he distrusts whatever seems sophistical. And yet the typical Wordsworth poem is based upon a paradoxical situation. Consider his celebrated

> It is a beauteous evening, calm and free,
> The holy time is quiet as a Nun
> Breathless with adoration. . . .

The poet is filled with worship, but the girl who walks beside him is not worshipping. The implication is that she should respond to the holy time, and become like the evening itself, nun-like; but she seems less worshipful than inanimate nature itself. Yet

> If thou appear untouched by solemn thought,
> Thy nature is not therefore less divine:
> Thou liest in Abraham's bosom all the year,
> And worship'st at the temple's inner shrine,
> God being with thee when we know it not.

The underlying paradox (of which the enthusiastic reader may well be unconscious) is nevertheless thoroughly necessary, even for that reader. Why does the innocent girl worship more deeply than the self-conscious poet who walks beside her? Because she is filled with an unconscious sympathy for *all* of nature, not merely the grandiose and solemn. One remembers the lines from Wordsworth's friend, Coleridge:

> He prayeth best, who loveth best
> All things both great and small.

Her unconscious sympathy is the unconscious worship. She is in communion with nature "all the year," and her devotion is continual whereas that of the poet is sporadic and momentary. But we have not done with the paradox yet. It not only underlies the poem, but something of the paradox informs the poem, though, since this is Wordsworth, rather timidly. The comparison of the evening to the nun actually has more than one dimension. The calm of the evening obviously means "worship," even to the dull-witted and insensitive. It corresponds to the trappings of the nun, visible to everyone. Thus, it suggests not merely holiness, but, in the total poem, even a hint of pharisaical holiness, with which the girl's careless innocence, itself a symbol of her continual secret worship, stands in contrast.

Or consider Wordsworth's sonnet, "Composed upon Westminster Bridge." I believe that most of us will agree that it is one of Wordsworth's most successful poems; yet most students have the greatest difficulty in accounting for its goodness. The attempt to account for it on the grounds of nobility of sentiment soon breaks down. On this level, the poem merely says: that the city in the morning light presents a picture which is majestic and touching to all but the most dull of soul; but the poem says very little more about the sight: the city is beautiful in the morning light and it is awfully still. The attempt to make a case for the poem in terms of the brilliance of its images also quickly breaks down: the student searches for graphic details in vain; there are next to no realistic touches. In fact, the poet simply huddles the details together:

> . . . silent, bare
> Ships, towers, domes, theatres, and temples lie
> Open unto the fields. . . .

We get a blurred impression—points of roofs and pinnacles along the skyline, all twinkling in the morning light. More than that, the sonnet as a whole contains some very flat writing and some well-worn comparisons.

The reader may ask: where, then, does the poem get its power? It gets it, it seems to me, from the paradoxical situation out of which the poem arises. Wordsworth is honestly surprised, and he manages to get some sense of awed surprise into the poem. It is odd to the poet that the city should be able to "wear the beauty of the morning" at all. Mount Snowden, Skiddaw, Mont Blanc—these wear it by natural right, but surely not grimy, feverish London. This is the point of the almost shocked exclamation

> Never did sun more beautifully steep
> In his first splendour, *valley, rock,* or *hill.* .

The "smokeless air" reveals a city which the poet did not know existed: man-made London is a part of nature too, is lighted by the sun of nature, and lighted to as beautiful effect.

The river glideth at his own sweet will. . .

A river is the most "natural" thing that one can imagine; it has the elasticity, the curved line of nature itself. The poet had never been able to regard this one as a real river—now, uncluttered by barges, the river reveals itself as a natural thing, not at all disciplined into a rigid and mechanical pattern: it is like the daffodils, or the mountain brooks, artless, and whimsical, and "natural" as they. The poem closes, you will remember, as follows:

> Dear God! the very houses seem asleep;
> And all that mighty heart is lying still!

The city, in the poet's insight of the morning, has earned its right to be considered organic, not merely mechanical. That is why the stale metaphor of the sleeping houses is strangely renewed. The most exciting thing that the poet can say about the houses is that they are *asleep*. He has been in the habit of counting them dead—as just mechanical and inanimate; to say they are "asleep" is to say that they are alive, that they participate in the life of nature. In the same way, the tired old metaphor which sees a great city as a pulsating heart of empire becomes revivified. It is only when the poet sees the city under the semblance of death that he can see it as actually alive—quick with the only life which he can accept, the organic life of "nature."

It is not my intention to exaggerate Wordsworth's own consciousness of the paradox involved. In this poem, he prefers, as is usual with him, the frontal attack. But the situation is paradoxical here as in so many of his poems. In his preface to the second edition of the *Lyrical Ballads* Wordsworth stated that his general purpose was "to choose incidents and situations from common life" but so to treat them that "ordinary things should be presented to the mind in an unusual aspect." Coleridge was to state the purpose for him later, in terms which make even more evident Wordsworth's exploitation of the paradoxical: "Mr. Wordsworth . . . was to propose to himself as his object, to give the charm of novelty to things of every day, and to excite a feeling analogous to the supernatural, by awakening the mind's attention to the lethargy of custom, and directing it to the loveliness and the wonders of the world before us. . . . " Wordsworth in short was consciously attempting to show his audience that the common was really uncommon, the prosaic was really poetic.

Coleridge's terms, "the charm of novelty to things of every day," "awakening the mind," suggest the Romantic preoccupation with wonder—the surprise, the revelation which puts the tarnished familiar world in a new light. This may well be the *raison d'etre* of most Romantic paradoxes; and yet the neoclassic poets use paradox for much the same reason. Consider Pope's lines from "The Essay on Man":

In doubt his Mind or Body to prefer;
Born but to die, and reas'ning but to err;

Alike in ignorance, his Reason such,
Whether he thinks too little, or too much. . . .

Created half to rise, and half to fall;
Great Lord of all things, yet a Prey to all;
Sole Judge of Truth, in endless Error hurl'd;
The Glory, Jest, and Riddle of the world!

Here, it is true, the paradoxes insist on the irony, rather than on the wonder. But Pope too might have claimed that he was treating the things of every day, man himself, and awakening his mind so that he would view himself in a new and blinding light. Thus, there is a certain awed wonder in Pope just as there is a certain trace of irony implicit in the Wordsworth sonnets. There is, of course, no reason why they should not occur together; and they do. Wonder and irony merge in many of the lyrics of Blake; they merge in Coleridge's *Ancient Mariner*. The variations in emphasis are numerous. Gray's "Elegy" uses a typical Wordsworth "situation" with the rural scene and with peasants contemplated in the light of their "betters." But in the "Elegy" the balance is heavily tilted in the direction of irony, the revelation an ironic rather than a startling one:

Can storied urn or animated bust
Back to its mansion call the fleeting breath?
Can Honour's voice provoke the silent dust,
Or Flatt'ry sooth the dull cold ear of Death?

But I am not here interested in the possible variations; I am interested rather in our seeing that the paradoxes spring from the very nature of the poet's language: it is a language in which the connotations play as great a part as the denotations. And I do not mean that the connotations are important as supplying some sort of frill or trimming, something external to the real matter in hand. I mean that the poet does not use a notation at all—as the scientist may properly be said to do so. The poet, within limits, has to make up his language as he goes.

T. S. Eliot somewhere refers to "that perpetual slight alteration of language, words perpetually juxtaposed in new and sudden combinations," which occurs in poetry. It *is* perpetual; it cannot be kept out of the poem; it can only be directed and controlled. The tendency of science is necessarily to stabilize terms, to freeze them into strict denotations; the poet's tendency is by contrast disruptive. His terms are continually modifying each other, and thus violating their dictionary meanings. To take a very simple example, consider the adjectives in the first lines of Wordsworth's evening sonnet: *beauteous, calm, free, holy, quiet, breathless*. The juxtapositions are hardly startling; and yet notice this: the evening is like a nun breathless with adoration. The adjective "breathless" suggests tremendous excitement; and yet the evening is not only quiet but *calm*. There is no final contradiction, to be sure: it is *that* kind of calm and *that* kind of excitement, and the two states may well occur together. But the poet has no one term. Even if he had a polysyllabic technical term, the term would not provide the solution for his prob-lem. He must work by contradiction and qualification.

We may approach the problem in this way: the poet has to work by analogies. All of the subtler states of emotion, as I. A. Richards has pointed out, neces-sarily demand metaphor for their expression. The poet must work by analogies, but the metaphors do not lie in the same plane or fit neatly edge to edge. There is a continual tilting of the planes; necessary overlappings, discrepancies, contradictions. Even the most direct and simple poet is forced into paradoxes far more often than we think, if we are sufficiently alive to what he is doing.*

But in dilating on the difficulties of the poet's task, I do not want to leave the impression that it is a task which necessarily defeats him, or even that with his

* All metaphor, of course, involves some element of paradox, for metaphor by its very nature cannot give a strictly point-to-point analogy with no element of discrepancy and contradiction between the items compared. Indeed, even Dr. Johnson drew the line in practice far short of general agreement between the items compared: he refused to allow that Addison's famous angel simile was a real simile. Marlborough directing the battle and the angel directing the storm were too closely parallel. The items compared—the tenor and the vehicle—had to "contradict" each other sharply, and in this contradiction lies the element of paradox which this paper attempts to emphasize. For the strat-egy of this paper, I have felt justified in making such an em-phasis. But it is only fair to say that I should prefer as a matter of general practice to approach many of the problems raised in this paper as problems of metaphor; that is, I have no desire to force the application of the term "paradox" on every case of discrepancy.

method he may not win to a fine precision. To use Shakespeare's figure, he can

> with assays of bias
> By indirections find directions out.

Shakespeare had in mind the game of lawnbowls in which the bowl is distorted, a circumstance which allows the skilful player to bowl a curve. To elaborate the figure, science makes use of the perfect sphere and its attack can be direct. The method of art can, I believe, never be direct—is always indirect. But that does not mean that the master of the game cannot place the bowl where he wants it. The serious difficulties will occur only when he confuses his game with that of science and mistakes the nature of his appropriate instrument. Mr. Stuart Chase a few years ago, with a touching naïveté, urged us to take the distortion out of the bowl—to treat language like notation.

I have said that even the apparently simple and straightforward poet is forced into paradoxes by the nature of his instrument. Seeing this, we should not be surprised to find poets who consciously employ it to gain a compression and precision otherwise unobtainable. Such a method, like any other, carries with it its own perils. But the dangers are not overpowering; the poem is not predetermined to a shallow and glittering sophistry. The method is an extension of the normal language of poetry, not a perversion of it.

I should like to refer you to a concrete case. Donne's "Canonization" ought to provide a sufficiently extreme instance.

For Godsake hold your tongue, and let me love,
    Or chide my palsie, or my gout,
My five gray haires, or ruin'd fortune flout,
    With wealth your state, your minde with Arts
        improve,
      Take you a course, get you a place,
      Observe his honour, or his grace,
Or the Kings reall, or his stamped face
      Contemplate, what you will, approve,
      So you will let me love.

Alas, alas, who's injur'd by my love?
    What merchants ships have my sighs drown'd?
Who saies my teares have overflow'd his ground?
    When did my colds a forward spring remove?
      When did the heats which my veines fill
      Adde one more to the plaguie Bill?
Soldiers finde warres, and Lawyers finde out still
      Litigious men, which quarrels move,
      Though she and I do love.

Call us what you will, wee are made such by love;
    Call her one, mee another flye,
We'are Tapers too, and at our owne cost die,
    And wee in us finde the'Eagle and the Dove.
      The Phoenix ridle hath more wit
      By us, we two being one, are it.
So to one neutrall thing both sexes fit,
      We dye and rise the same, and prove
      Mysterious by this love.

Wee can dye by it, if not live by love,
    And if unfit for tombes and hearse
Our legend bee, it will be fit for verse;
    And if no peece of Chronicle wee prove,

We'll build in sonnets pretty roomes;
As well a well wrought urne becomes
The greatest ashes, as halfe-acre tombes,
And by these hymnes, all shall approve
Us Canoniz'd for Love:

And thus invoke us; You whom reverend love
Made one anothers hermitage;
You, to whom love was peace, that now is rage;
Who did the whole worlds soule contract, and
drove
Into the glasses of your eyes
(So made such mirrors, and such spies,
That they did all to you epitomize,)
Countries, Townes, Courts: Beg from above
A patterne of your love!

The basic metaphor which underlies the poem (and
which is reflected in the title) involves a sort of paradox. For the poet daringly treats profane love as if it
were divine love. The canonization is not that of a
pair of holy anchorites who have renounced the world
and the flesh. The hermitage of each is the other's
body; but they do renounce the world, and so their
title to sainthood is cunningly argued. The poem then
is a parody of Christian sainthood; but it is an in-
tensely serious parody of a sort that modern man,
habituated as he is to an easy yes or no, can hardly
understand. He refuses to accept the paradox as a
serious rhetorical device; and since he is able to accept
it only as a cheap trick, he is forced into this dilemma.
Either: Donne does not take love seriously; here he
is merely sharpening his wit as a sort of mechanical

exercise. Or: Donne does not take sainthood seriously; here he is merely indulging in a cynical and bawdy parody.

Neither account is true; a reading of the poem will show that Donne takes both love and religion seriously; it will show, further, that the paradox is here his inevitable instrument. But to see this plainly will require a closer reading than most of us give to poetry.

The poem opens dramatically on a note of exasperation. The "you" whom the speaker addresses is not identified. We can imagine that it is a person, perhaps a friend, who is objecting to the speaker's love affair. At any rate, the person represents the practical world which regards love as a silly affectation. To use the metaphor on which the poem is built, the friend represents the secular world which the lovers have renounced.

Donne begins to suggest this metaphor in the first stanza by the contemptuous alternatives which he suggests to the friend

> . . . chide my palsy, or my gout,
> My five gray haires, or ruin'd fortune flout . . .

The implications are: (1) All right, consider my love as an infirmity, as a disease, if you will, but confine yourself to my other infirmities, my palsy, my approaching old age, my ruined fortune. You stand a better chance of curing those; in chiding me for this one, you are simply wasting your time as well as mine. (2) Why don't you pay attention to your own welfare

—go on and get wealth and honor for yourself. What should you care if I do give these up in pursuing my love?

The two main categories of secular success are neatly, and contemptuously epitomized in the line

Or the Kings reall, or his stamped face.

Cultivate the court and gaze at the king's face there, or, if you prefer, get into business and look at his face stamped on coins. But let me alone.

This conflict between the "real" world and the lover absorbed in the world of love runs through the poem; it dominates the second stanza in which the torments of love, so vivid to the lover, affect the real world not at all—

What merchants ships have my sighs drown'd?

It is touched on in the fourth stanza in the contrast between the word "Chronicle" which suggests secular history with its pomp and magnificence, the history of kings and princes, and the word "sonnets" with its suggestions of trivial and precious intricacy. The conflict appears again in the last stanza, only to be resolved when the unworldly lovers, love's saints who have given up the world, paradoxically achieve a more intense world. But here the paradox is still contained in, and supported by, the dominant metaphor: so does the holy anchorite win a better world by giving up this one.

But before going on to discuss this development of the theme, it is important to see what else the second stanza does. For it is in this second stanza and the third, that the poet shifts the tone of the poem, modulating from the note of irritation with which the poem opens into the quite different tone with which it closes.

Donne accomplishes the modulation of tone by what may be called an analysis of love-metaphor. Here, as in many of his poems, he shows that he is thoroughly self-conscious about what he is doing. This second stanza he fills with the conventionalized figures of the Petrarchan tradition: the wind of lovers' sighs, the floods of lovers' tears, etc.—extravagant figures with which the contemptuous secular friend might be expected to tease the lover. The implication is that the poet himself recognizes the absurdity of the Petrarchan love metaphors. But what of it? The very absurdity of the jargon which lovers are expected to talk makes for his argument: their love, however absurd it may appear to the world, does no harm to the world. The practical friend need have no fears: there will still be wars to fight and lawsuits to argue.

The opening of the third stanza suggests that this vein of irony is to be maintained. The poet points out to his friend the infinite fund of such absurdities which can be applied to lovers:

> Call her one, mee another flye,
> We'are Tapers too, and at our owne cost die . . .

For that matter, the lovers can conjure up for themselves plenty of such fantastic comparisons: *they* know what the world thinks of them. But these figures of the third stanza are no longer the threadbare Petrarchan conventionalities; they have sharpness and bite. The last one, the likening of the lovers to the phoenix, is fully serious, and with it, the tone has shifted from ironic banter into a defiant but controlled tenderness.

The effect of this implied awareness of the lovers' apparent madness is to cleanse and revivify metaphor; to indicate the sense in which the poet accepts it, and thus to prepare us for accepting seriously the fine and seriously intended metaphors which dominate the last two stanzas of the poem.

The opening line of the fourth stanza,

> Wee can dye by it, if not live by love,

achieves an effect of tenderness and deliberate resolution. The lovers are ready to die to the world; they are committed; they are not callow but confident. (The basic metaphor of the saint, one notices, is being carried on; the lovers in their renunciation of the world, have something of the confident resolution of the saint. By the bye, the word "legend"—

> . . . if unfit for tombes and hearse
> Our legend bee—

in Donne's time meant "the life of a saint.") The lovers are willing to forego the ponderous and stately chronicle and to accept the trifling and insubstantial "sonnet" instead; but then if the urn be well-wrought it provides a finer memorial for one's ashes than does the pompous and grotesque monument. With the finely contemptuous, yet quiet phrase, "half-acre tombes," the world which the lovers reject expands into something gross and vulgar. But the figure works further; the pretty sonnets will not merely hold their ashes as a decent earthly memorial. Their legend, their story, will gain them canonization; and approved as love's saints, other lovers will invoke them.

In this last stanza, the theme receives a final complication. The lovers in rejecting life actually win to the most intense life. This paradox has been hinted at earlier in the phoenix metaphor. Here it receives a powerful dramatization. The lovers in becoming hermits, find that they have not lost the world, but have gained the world in each other, now a more intense, more meaningful world. Donne is not content to treat the lovers' discovery as something which comes to them passively, but rather as something which they actively achieve. They are like the saint, God's athlete:

> Who did the whole worlds soule *contract,* and *drove*
> Into the glasses of your eyes. . . .

The image is that of a violent squeezing as of a powerful hand. And what do the lovers "drive" into each other's eyes? The "Countries, Townes," and "Courts," which they renounced in the first stanza of the poem. The unworldly lovers thus become the most "worldly" of all.

The tone with which the poem closes is one of triumphant achievement, but the tone is a development contributed to by various earlier elements. One of the more important elements which works toward our acceptance of the final paradox is the figure of the phoenix, which will bear a little further analysis.

The comparison of the lovers to the phoenix is very skilfully related to the two earlier comparisons, that in which the lovers are like burning tapers, and that in which they are like the eagle and the dove. The phoenix comparison gathers up both: the phoenix is a bird, and like the tapers, it burns. We have a selected series of items: the phoenix figure seems to come in a natural stream of association. "Call us what you will," the lover says, and rattles off in his desperation the first comparisons that occur to him. The comparison to the phoenix seems thus merely another outlandish one, the most outrageous of all. But it is this most fantastic one, stumbled over apparently in his haste, that the poet goes on to develop. It really describes the lovers best and justifies their renunciation. For the phoenix is not two but one, "we two being one, are it"; and it burns, not like the taper at its own cost, but to live again. Its death is life: "Wee dye and rise the same. . . ." The poet literally justifies the fantastic assertion. In the sixteenth and seventeenth centuries to "die" means to experience the consummation of the act of love. The lovers after the act are the same. Their love is not exhausted in mere lust. This is their title to canonization. Their love is like the phoenix.

I hope that I do not seem to juggle the meaning of *die*. The meaning that I have cited can be abundantly justified in the literature of the period; Shakespeare uses "die" in this sense; so does Dryden. Moreover, I do not think that I give it undue emphasis. The word is in a crucial position. On it is pivoted the transition to the next stanza,

> Wee can dye by it, if not live by love,
> And if unfit for tombes. . . .

Most important of all, the sexual submeaning of "die" does not contradict the other meanings: the poet is saying: "Our death is really a more intense life"; "We can afford to trade life (the world) for death (love), for that death is the consummation of life"; "After all, one does not expect to live *by* love, one expects, and wants, to die *by* it." But in the total passage he is also saying "Because our love is not mundane, we can give up the world"; "because our love is not merely lust, we can give up the other lusts, the lust for wealth and power"; "because," and this is said with a little vein of irony as by one who knows the world too well, "because our love can outlast its consummation, we are a minor miracle; we are love's saints." This passage with its ironical tenderness and its realism feeds and supports the brilliant paradox with which the poem closes.

There is one more factor in developing and sustaining the final effect. The poem is an instance of the doctrine which it asserts; it is both the assertion and the realization of the assertion. The poet has actually before our eyes built within the song the "pretty room" with which he says the lovers can be content. The poem itself is the well-wrought urn which can hold the lovers' ashes and which will not suffer in comparison with the prince's "half-acre tomb."

And how necessary are the paradoxes? Donne might have said directly, "Love in a cottage is enough." "The Canonization" contains this admirable thesis, but it contains a great deal more. He might have been as forthright as a later lyricist who wrote, "We'll build a sweet little nest, / Somewhere out in the West, / And let the rest of the world go by." He might even have imitated that more metaphysical lyric, which maintains, "You're the cream in my coffee." "The Canonization" touches on all these observations, but it goes beyond them, not merely in dignity, but in precision.

I submit that the only way by which the poet could say what "The Canonization" says is by paradox. More direct methods may be tempting, but all of them enfeeble and distort what is to be said. This statement may seem the less surprising when we reflect on how many of the important things which the poet has to say have to be said by means of paradox:—most of the language of lovers is such; "The Canonization" is a good example; most of the language of religion: "He who would save his life, must lose it"; "The last shall be first." Indeed, almost any insight important enough to warrant a great poem apparently has to be stated in such terms. Deprived of the character of paradox with its twin concomitants of

irony and wonder, the matter of Donne's poem un-
ravels into "facts," biological, sociological, and economic. What happens to Donne's lovers if we consider them "scientifically," without benefit of the
supernaturalism which the poet confers upon them?*
Well, what happens to Shakespeare's lovers, for

* In this paper I have not attempted to distinguish between
kinds of paradoxes. Obviously, they do not stand on the same
level: for example, there are doctrinal paradoxes such as the
Christian mystery of the Trinity; there are philosophical paradoxes such as are found in Kant's antinomies; there are rhetorical paradoxes, themselves of innumerable kinds. An elaborate
classification of types would be out of place in a paper of this
sort; nor have I cared to take up here the problem of the relation
of poetry to philosophy and religion. But the statement that the
poet confers upon facts a "supernaturalism" does call for further
comment. Perhaps something like "super-positivism" should be
substituted for "supernaturalism." The point that I have in mind
is related to the discussion of positivism in Mr. Allen Tate's recent *Reason in Madness*: "There are 'two doctrines,' [I. A. Rich-
ards] says, which have tended to flourish independently—" and
yet, neither is intelligible apart from Imagination.

"The two doctrines can be stated as follows:

"1. The mind of the poet at moments . . . gains an insight into
reality, reads Nature as a symbol of something behind or within
Nature not ordinarily perceived.

"2. The mind of the poet creates a Nature into which his own
feelings, his aspirations and apprehensions, are projected."

"Now," continues Mr. Tate, "the positivist sciences have denied
all validity to the first doctrine." The poet is left, consequently,
to "project" his fancies. They have no objective validity. Yet
the world in which we live (not to be confused with the abstrac-
tions from it made by the various sciences) requires both the
first *and* second doctrine. It is a concrete world in which man
requires the "complete knowledge" which Mr. Tate holds that
poetry gives. And yet the two doctrines constitute a pair of
antinomies which can be reconciled only in the doctrine of the
Imagination to which Richards refers. The whole passage in
Reason and Madness and the chapter of Richards' *Coleridge on
Imagination* there discussed should be read in this connection.

Shakespeare uses the basic metaphor of "The Canonization" in his *Romeo and Juliet?* In their first conversation, you remember, the lovers play with the analogy between the lover and the pilgrim to the Holy Land. Juliet says:

> For saints have hands that pilgrims' hands do touch
> And palm to palm is holy palmers' kiss.

Considered scientifically, the lovers become Mr. Aldous Huxley's animals, "quietly sweating, palm to palm."

For us today, Donne's imagination seems obsessed with the problem of unity: the sense in which the lovers become one—the sense in which the soul is united with God. Frequently, as we have seen, one type of union becomes a metaphor for the other. It may not be too far-fetched to see both as instances of, and metaphors for, the union which the creative imagination itself effects. For that fusion is not logical; it apparently violates science and commonsense; it welds together the discordant and the contradictory. Coleridge has of course given us the classic description of its nature and power. It "reveals itself in the balance or reconcilement of opposite or discordant qualities: of sameness, with difference; of the general, with the concrete; the idea, with the image; the individual, with the representative; the sense of novelty and freshness, with old and familiar objects; a more than usual state of emotion, with more than usual order. . . ." It is a great and illuminating statement, but it is a series of paradoxes. Apparently Coleridge could describe the effect of the imagination in no other way.

Shakespeare, in one of his poems, has given a description that oddly parallels that of Coleridge.

> Reason in itself confounded,
> Saw Division grow together,
> To themselves yet either neither,
> Simple were so well compounded.

I do not know what his "The Phoenix and the Turtle" celebrates. Perhaps it *was* written to honor the marriage of Sir John Salisbury and Ursula Stanley; or perhaps the phoenix is Lucy, Countess of Bedford; or perhaps the poem is merely an essay on Platonic love. But the scholars themselves are so uncertain, that I think we will do little violence to established habits of thinking, if we boldly preempt the poem for our own purposes. Certainly the poem is an instance of that magic power which Coleridge sought to describe. I propose that we take it for a moment as a poem about that power:

> So they loved as love in twaine,
> Had the essence but in one,
> Two distincts, Division none,
> Number there in love was slaine.
>
> Hearts remote, yet not asunder;
> Distance and no space was seene,
> Twixt the *Turtle* and his Queene;
> But in them it were a wonder. . . .

> Propertie was thus appalled,
> That the selfe was not the same;
> Single Natures double name,
> Neither two nor one was called.

Precisely! The nature is single, one, unified. But the name is double, and today with our multiplication of sciences, it is multiple. If the poet is to be true to his poetry, he must call it neither two nor one: the paradox is his only solution. The difficulty has intensified since Shakespeare's day: the timid poet, when confronted with the problem of "Single Natures double name," has too often funked it. A history of poetry from Dryden's time to our own might bear as its subtitle "The Half-Hearted Phoenix."

In Shakespeare's poem, you will remember that at the union of the phoenix and the turtle, Reason is "in itselfe confounded"; but it recovers to admit its own bankruptcy,

> Love hath Reason, Reason none,
> If what parts, can so remaine. . . .

and it is Reason which goes on to utter the beautiful threnos with which the poem concludes:

> Beautie, Truth, and Raritie,
> Grace in all simplicitie,
> Here enclosede, in cinders lie. . . .
>
> Truth may seem, but cannot be;
> Beauty brag, but 'tis not she;
> Truth and beauty buried be.
>
> To this urne let those repaire,
> That are either true or faire,
> For these dead Birds, sigh a prayer.

Having preempted the poem for our own purposes, it may not be too outrageous to go on to deduce one further observation. The urn to which we are summoned, the urn which holds the ashes of the phoenix, is like the well-wrought urn of Donne's "Canonization" which holds the phoenix-lovers' ashes; it is the poem itself. One is reminded of still another urn, Keats's Grecian urn, which contained for Keats, Truth and Beauty as Shakespeare's urn encloses "Beautie, Truth, and Raritie." But there is a sense in which all such well-wrought urns contain the ashes of a phoenix. The urns are not meant for memorial purposes only, though that often seems to be their chief significance to the professors of literature. The phoenix rises from its ashes; or ought to rise; but it will not arise merely for our sifting and measuring the ashes, or testing them for their chemical content. We must be prepared to accept the paradox of the imagination itself; else "Beautie, Truth, and Raritie" remain enclosed in their cinders and we shall end with essential cinders, for all our pains.

THE INTERACTIONS OF WORDS

BY I. A. RICHARDS

THE INTERACTIONS OF WORDS

I. A. RICHARDS

*T*HERE SHOULD BE an ancient saying, "If you talk too much about words, your tongue will become a stone." More than once in this lecture you will see why. I have been minded again and again to change my title or dodge the topic "Whereof we cannot speak, thereof we must be silent," remarked Ludwig Wittgenstein some twenty years ago, but men have gone on inventing languages in which to talk about that silence.

What are these words we talk with and talk so much about? Taking poetry to be an affair of the interaction of words, how far will we get in a discussion of poetry if we are in real doubt about what words are and do?

This essay threatens thus to become an attempt to define "a word." I am extremely loath to inflict that upon you. The definition of "a word" has been a task from which the best authorities have rightly shrunk, an obligation which had made even psychologists into mystics and left the adepts in linguistics at a loss. But when the subject has been tactlessly raised, how are we to avoid it? How are we to conceive the interactions of words without forming as clear a conception as we can of the words themselves?

"As clear a conception as we can!" But what are these *conceptions* and how can they be *clear?* The implications of this word "conception," if we take it literally and thereby awaken it to full metaphoric liveliness, are a philosophy of poetic language—as Plato pointed out, in the *Phaedrus* (277). It is true he calls them "scientific words" there, but he was concerned with "the dialectic art" which I arbitrarily take here to have been the practice of a supreme sort of poetry —the sort which was to replace the poetry he banished from the Republic. Here is the passage. "Noble it may be to tell stories about justice and virtue; but far nobler is a man's work, when finding a congenial soul he avails himself of the dialectic art to sow and plant therein scientific words, which are competent to defend themselves, and him who planted them, and are not unfruitful, but bear seed in their turn, from which other words springing up in other minds are capable of preserving this precious seed ever undecaying, and making their possessor ever happy, so far as happiness is possible to man." Plato is fond of this sort of language. If you look for it you will find it everywhere in the *Republic,* used with a frankness which embarrassed his Victorian translators.

What are these conceptions through which words, by uniting, bring new beings into the world, or new worlds into being? A truly philosophic definition of "a word" would be, I suppose, an all-purposes definition. I am hoping for no such thing—only for a definition useful for our purpose: the study of the language of poetry. But limits to that are not easily set. However, I can escape some of the most dreadful parts of the undertaking by assuming frankly that our purposes are not those of psychology or of linguistics. Their troubles come in part from the uses for which they require their definitions of "a word." Poetics has a different set of purposes and needs a different sort of definition. If so, I can work at it without the tedious attempt to relate it to the other definitions that other studies need. Philosophically speaking, this leaves Poetics "up in the air"; but that is perhaps where, in the present state of philosophy, it will be safest.

But very likely someone will already be saying, "Wait a moment. Are these troubles real or only philosophic? Do we really need any definition poetic or otherwise? Are not most of us in fact clear enough about what poetry and words in general are and do? This marvellous, this miraculous thing we call our language works somehow for us and within us; the better, it may well be, for our not knowing too much about it. Our digestions, to take a humble parallel, do not depend, fortunately, on our knowledge of physiology. Don't our poetic difficulties also arise with particular instances only? Isn't this pretence that we never understand what we are saying or how we say it rather like witchcraft—an epidemic invented to give employment to specialists in its treatment?"

"I would meet you upon this honestly." Such questionings can be barren. To ask "What is a word and

how does it work?" may do us no good. On the other
hand, there is a sense in which this question is the very
foundation, the source, the origin, the ἀρχή (to use
Plato's word), the starting point and final cause of
the intellectual life. But I do not know how, *in words,*
to distinguish the idle from the vital question here.

In the philosophy of poetry this vital question is
not a question of fact but one of choice or decision.
In that, it is like the fundamental definitions of mathe-
matics. Facts, by themselves, do not, in any simple
direct way, settle what we should define "a word" to
be. Facts, which we are aware of and can compare
only through words, come later. None the less our
definition must let the facts be facts. We do well to
be humble here; this "What is a word?" is one of the
founding questions—along with "What am I?"
"What is a fact?" and "What is God?"—on which all
other questions balance and turn. The art of entertain-
ing such questions, and of distinguishing them from
other questions which we might ask with the same
sounds, is the dialectic study of poetry. And the
founding questions—those that establish and main-
tain our state as men—are themselves poetic. But that
might mean so many false things that I tremble as I
say it.

Still, the other ways of saying it, and ways of
guarding it, suffer equal danger. If I add, for example, that this poetic basis of ours is no matter of
mere make-believe, well, we have the varying possible
ways of understanding that richly mysterious phrase,

"make-believe," before us. "Mere make-believe."
Here is a notable example of the interaction of words.
Just where do its disparaging or mocking implications
come from? Are beliefs *not* to be made (i.e. forced)?
Is *that* the point? Or is it the poor quality of the belief
so made? Are beliefs which *we* make not genuine?
Must the world, something not ourselves, make them
for us? And if so, *which* world will we trust to do
that? The world of tradition, of theology, of current
public opinion, of science, or one of the worlds of
poetry? Which will give us the beliefs we need? Is
that the question, or is it the inferior quality of such
beliefs which is being mocked, the immature crafts-
manship, the inexperience which knows too little
about either the materials or the purpose of the belief?

All this and more is to be considered in asking
seriously if the poetic basis of our world is make-
believe. This phrase, *make-believe,* like a good watch
dog, warns us off sternly—if we have no proper business with these premises. But if we were their master,
it would be silent. There is another possibility of
course. In the Chinese story the stone-deaf visitor
remarked, "Why do you keep your dog up so late?
He did nothing but yawn at me as I came through
the gate."

However, if we know what we are doing, and what
the phrase "make-believe" is doing—and it has several senses which should alarm us for one which is
safe because true—we may say that our world rests
on make-belief or—to use a more venerable word—

on faith. But it is *our* world, mind you, which so rests, our world in which we live as men, so different from the bullet's world, in which *it* travels. And yet our world includes the bullet.

I have been trying with all this to revive for you the sense of the word "maker," in which a poet may be seriously said to be a maker. This is the sense in which poetry matters because it is creative—not the sense in which we say it is "creative" because we feel it matters. The poet is a maker of beliefs—but do not give here to "belief" the first meaning that comes to mind, for it is as true that for other senses of "belief" poetry has nothing to do with them. What does the poet *make* and what does his work *create?* Himself and his world first, and thereby other worlds and other men. He makes through shaping and molding, through giving form. But if we ask what he shapes or molds or gives form to, we must answer with Aristotle that we can say nothing about that which has no form. There are always prior forms upon which the poet works, and how he takes these forms is part of his making. He apprehends them by taking them into forms of more comprehensive order. To the poet as poet, his world is the world, and the world is his world. But the poet is not always poet. All but the greatest poets in the most favorable societies seem to have to pay for being poets. Of recent poets, Yeats has put this best:

The intellect of man is forced to choose
Perfection of the life or of the work,

And if it take the second must refuse
A heavenly mansion, raging in the dark.
When all that story's finished, what's the news?
In luck or out, the toil has left its mark:
That old perplexity, an empty purse
Or the day's vanity, the night's remorse.

The work of the poet is the maintenance and enlargement of the human spirit through remaking it under changing circumstances; through molding and remolding the ever-varying flux. The molds are sets of words, interacting in manifold ways within a language. At first sight this old Platonic image of the mold looks crude. What could be less like a mold than a word—which endlessly changes its work with its company as we all may note if we care to look? But the mold metaphor—the dominant metaphor of the Greek invention of education—is there to shock us into thought. The poetic problem is precisely the maintenance of stability *within* minds and correspondence *between* them. It is *not* how to get the flux into molds supposed somehow to be fixed already; but how to recreate perpetually those constancies (as of sets of molds) upon which depend any order, any growth, any development—any changes, in fact, other than the chance-ridden changes of chaos.

It is through the interactions of words within a language that a poet works. In a sense all literary men are inquiring concretely into the detail of this in all their work, but let us try to take a more general and comprehensive view before going on to contrast two types of verbal interactions. If I can show you how I conceive words, the rest will be easier. First I spoke of the *question,* "What is a word?", not of any answer to it, as one of the founding forces, and as thereby poetic. Answers to it of many sorts can be contrived and offered. Linguistics and psychology in their different divisions have many very different answers and the debate between them, as studies aspiring to become sciences (in various senses of "science") must be a long one. But these answers would answer different questions from my poetic "What is a word?" That question is nourished by awareness of them, but it is not reducible to them. It is not answered by an exhaustive dictionary or encyclopedia article on the word *Word.* That would answer only the set of historical, factual, linguistic, psychological, religious, metaphysical and other questions which I am trying —by these very odd means—to distinguish from the poetic question. With any of these questions, it would be shocking—would it not?—to suggest that its answer is one and the same with itself. But the poetic question has to be its own answer—as virtue is its own reward, to cite the wider rule of which this is an example. As an answer it is aware that it is a bundle of possibilities dependent on other possibilities which in turn it in part determines; as a question it is attempting through its influence on them to become more completely itself. It is growing as a cell grows

· 72 ·

with other cells. It is a conception. It is being "divided at the joints" and recombined. "Attempting" and "growing" are not metaphors here. A word, a question or its answer, does all that we do, since we do all that in the word. Words are alive as our other acts are alive—though apart from the minds which use them they are nothing but agitations of the air or stains on paper.

A word then by this sort of definition is a permanent set of possibilities of understanding, much as John Stuart Mill's table was a permanent possibility of sensation. And as the sensations the table yields depend on the angle you look from, the other things you see it with, the air, your glasses, your eyes and the light . . . so how a word is understood depends on the other words you hear it with, and the other frames you have heard it in, on the whole setting present and past in which it has developed as a part of your mind. But the interactions of words with one another and with other things are far more complex than can be paralleled from the case of the table—complex enough as those are. Indeed they are not paralleled anywhere except by such things as pictures, music or the expressions of faces which are other modes of language. Language, as understood, is the mind itself at work and these interactions of words are interdependencies of our own being.

I conceive then a word, as poetry is concerned with it, and as separated from the mere physical or sensory occasion, to be a component of an act of the mind so subtly dependent on the other components of this act and of other acts that it can be distinguished from these interactions only as a convenience of discourse. It sounds nonsense to say that a word is its interactions with other words; but that is a short way of saying the thing which Poetics is in most danger always of overlooking. Words only work together. We understand no word except in and through its interactions with other words.

Let me now come down to detail. I invite you to compare two very different types of the interactions of words in poetry: I will read the first twelve lines of Donne's *First Anniversary*.

AN ANATOMY OF THE WORLD
THE FIRST ANNIVERSARY

Wherein

By reason of the untimely death of Mistress
Elizabeth Drury, the frailty and the decay
of this whole world is represented.

When that rich Soule which to her heaven is gone,
Whom all do celebrate, who know they have one,
(For who is sure he hath a Soule, unlesse
It see, and judge, and follow worthinesse,
And by Deedes praise it? hee who doth not this,
May lodge an In-mate soule, but 'tis not his.)

When that Queene ended here her progresse time,
And, as t'her standing house to heaven did climbe,
Where loath to make the Saints attend her long,
She's now a part both of the Quire, and Song,
This world, in that great earthquake languished;
For in a common bath of teares it bled.

Let us compare with that the first stanza of Dryden's
*Ode: To the Pious Memory of the accomplished
young lady, Mrs. Anne Killigrew, excellent
in the two sister arts of Poesy and Painting*

Thou youngest virgin-daughter of the skies,
Made in the last promotion of the blest;
Whose palms, new pluck'd from Paradise,
In spreading branches more sublimely rise,
Rich with immortal green above the rest:
Whether, adopted to some neighboring star,
Thou roll'st above us, in thy wandering race,
Or, in procession fixt and regular,
Mov'd with the heaven's majestic pace;
Or, call'd to more superior bliss,
Thou tread'st with seraphims the vast abyss:
Whatever happy region is thy place,
Cease thy celestial song a little space;
Thou wilt have time enough for hymns divine,
Since Heaven's eternal year is thine.
Hear, then, a mortal Muse thy praise rehearse,
In no ignoble verse;
But such as thy own voice did practice here,
When thy first-fruits of Poesy were given,
To make thyself a welcome inmate there;
While yet a young probationer,
And candidate of Heaven.

· 75 ·

In the Donne, I suggest, there is a prodigious activity between the words as we read them. Following, exploring, realizing, *becoming* that activity is, I suggest, the essential thing in reading the poem. Understanding it is not a preparation for reading the poem. It is itself the poem. And it is a constructive, hazardous, free creative process, a process of conception through which a new being is growing in the mind. The Dryden, I suggest, is quite otherwise. No doubt there are interactions between the words but they are on a different level. The words are in routine conventional relations like peaceful diplomatic communications between nations. They do not induce revolutions in one another and are not thereby attempting to form a new order. Any mutual adjustments they have to make are preparatory, and they are no important part of the poetic activity. In brief Dryden's poem comes before our minds as a mature creation. But we seem to create Donne's poem.

Donne's poem is called *The First Anniversary* because he wrote it a year after the death of Elizabeth Drury. He was going to write a similar poem every year but only wrote one other. His latest editor, Mr. John Hayward (in the Nonesuch Edition) says this "concluded the series of preposterous eulogies." Whether Mr. Hayward thinks them preposterous, whether they are eulogies, and whether, if we took them as such, they would be preposterous—are questions I leave till later.

Opinion about them has always been mixed. Ben Jonson is reported to have said that "they were prophane and full of blasphemies; that he told Mr. Donne if it had been written of the Virgin Marie it had been something; to which he answered that he described the Idea of a Woman, and not as she was." That is a helpful hint. It points to the Platonism in the poem. But Mr. Hayward comments: "However this may be, the subject of the two poems was a real woman, a child rather, who died in 1610 at the age of fifteen." Two things are worth a word here. Doubtless, in one sense, Elizabeth Drury is the subject; but in a more important sense, the subject of the poem, what it is about, is something which only a good reading will discover. That discovery here is the poetic process. Secondly, when Mr. Hayward says "a child rather," he is being twentieth century, not seventeenth century. A fifteen year old girl was a woman for the seventeenth century. In Donne's poem *Upon the Annunciation and the Passion* he writes of the Virgin Mary:

Sad and rejoyc'd shee's seen at once, and seen
At almost fiftie and at scarce fifteene.

For Donne the Annunciation came to Mary when she was "scarce fifteene." Elizabeth's youth is of course no bar—rather the reverse—to Donne's taking her very seriously as a symbol.

Dryden's *Ode* has long been an anthology piece. Dr. Johnson called it "the noblest Ode that our

Language produced" and "the richest complex of sounds in our language." A modern critic has called this "a judgment then bold but now scarcely intelligible." There are seventy-five years between the poems.

Now let us consider the lines in detail and especially this question, "How closely should we be examining them in our reading?" I will take Dryden first. You may guess perhaps that even in taking him first here I am expressing a judgment between them.

How near should we come to the *Ode*? The only way to find out is by experimenting. Public declamation—the style of reading which the *Ode* suggests as right—does not invite close attention to the meaning. The façade of a public building is not to be studied with a handglass. Gulliver, you remember, thought nothing of the complexions of the Brobdingnagian ladies. Let us try looking a little closer.

Thou youngest virgin-daughter of the skies

Why "youngest virgin-daughter"? "Youngest" may here mean "new-born"; but then, why *virgin*? New-borns are necessarily virgins. And why, then, "daughter of the skies"? Do we need especially to be reminded that daughters of the skies—in Christian mythology—as denizens of Paradise, are virgins? On earth she was a virgin, it is true. In Heaven, there is neither marriage nor giving in marriage. And there is no special relation to the Virgin. We gain nothing by such ponderings here.

Again:

> *Whose palms, new plucked from Paradise*
> *In spreading branches more sublimely rise*
> *Rich with immortal green above the rest.*

Why *from* Paradise? Has she left it? Why not *in* Paradise? The answer might be in terms of resonance of the line.

But why should these palms of hers *more sublimely* rise? or be "rich with immortal green *above the rest*"? Do Paradisaic palms wilt and fade like florist's goods here on earth? Or does the row of palms get greener and greener, richer and richer, loftier and loftier, as we get further along the line from the first saints?

Clearly these questions and all others of the sort are quite irrelevant and out of place. We are looking too close, looking for a kind of poetic structure, an interaction of the words which is not there and is not needed for the proper purpose of the poem.

The same thing would appear if we questioned similarly Dryden's suggestions about what she is doing and where she is: on a planet, "in thy wandering race" or on a fixed star "in procession fixt and regular." Or if we wondered whether "the vast abyss" so described seems a *happy* region. Or again if we ask whether she need really stop singing to listen to Dryden. Or again whether Dryden really, for a moment, considers her earthly verses to have been such as his own voice is practicing here? Of course, he doesn't. Or again, if we ask whether her *verses* could possibly make her welcome *in Paradise*? Or if they would advance her as a "candidate for heaven"? Or lastly if we asked why she is called an "inmate"? We shall see later that the same word in the Donne is packed with implications.

The outcome of all such close questioning is the same. Dryden's words have no such implications and we shall be misreading him if we hunt for them. In brief, this is not a poetry of Wit—in the technical sense of the word in which Donne's verses are, as Coleridge called them,

Wit's fire and fireblast, meaning's press and screw.

On this question of wit, let us listen to Dr. Johnson a moment. He is talking about conversation and has been comparing styles of conversation with beverages. He says,

"Spirit alone is too powerful to use. It will produce madness rather than merriment; and instead of quenching thirst, will inflame the blood. Thus wit, too copiously poured out, agitates the hearer with emotions rather violent than pleasing; everyone shrinks from the force of its oppression, the company sits entranced and overpowered; all are astonished, but nobody is pleased." One might retort, "Please, why should we please?" Or, when he says, "It will produce madness rather than merriment," we might recall the link between poetry and madness that has been noted from Plato's time to Shakespeare's. Dr.

Johnson had deep personal reasons for distrusting this connection. He would have replied that he was talking about conversation, social intercourse. "Instead of quenching thirst," he says, "wit will inflame the blood." Quenching thirst? "Do you converse, Sir, in order to have had enough of it?" But Dr. Johnson's prose here no more requires us to pursue such implications and interactions than Dryden's verses.

Turn now to the Donne. Let us see what minute reading brings out of that.

When that rich Soule which to her heaven is gone,

rich: in two senses—possessing much (a rich man); giving much (a rich mine). Compare Coleridge:

> Oh lady, we receive but what we give
> And in our life alone does Nature live.

or Croce: "Intuition is Expression": we *have* only that which we can give out.

her heaven: again the double force; she possesses it and it possesses her, as with "her country," or "her place."

Whom all do celebrate, who know they have one;

celebrate: a new word then in the sense of "praise, extol, or publish the fame of." This would be its first occurrence in that sense. Prior to 1611 it means "commemorate or perform publicly and in due form (with a ritual—as in a celebration of the Eucharist) or solemnize." There is a very serious suggestion of participation or partaking or ritual imitation. Thus, all who know they have a soul partake of that rich Soule, in knowing that (i.e. in having a soul). Then follows Donne's gloss:

> *For who is sure he hath a Soule, unlesse*
> *It see, and judge, and follow worthiness;*

sure is more than "confident, without doubts about it"; it means "safe, firm, immovable," because seeing, judging and following worthiness are themselves the very possession of a soul, not merely signs of having one. To see and judge and follow worthiness is to have a soul.

worthiness: excellence in the highest of all senses. That use was going out in Donne's time (1617).

> *And by Deedes praise it*

No verbal praise, but imitation of or participation in actual works;

> *He who doth not this,*
> *May lodge an In-mate soule, but 'tis not his.*

in-mate: a word of very ill suggestions. We keep some of them in "an inmate of a penitentiary or an asylum." For Donne it suggests a lodger or a foreigner. Compare Milton:

> So spake the Enemie of Mankind, enclos'd
> In Serpent, Inmate bad, (P.L. ix, 495)

Who does not see and follow worthiness hasn't a soul but is possessed by something not truly him.

As so often with Donne, what seems a most far-

fetched conceit is no more than the result of taking
a commonplace of language seriously. We say daily
that a man is "not himself" or "beside himself" or
"not his true self," and we do the same thing when
we say he is "alienated" or call a psychopathologist
an "alienist." Donne is just expanding such expressions, making their implications explicit, increasing
their interaction, as heat increases chemical interaction. That is the technique of most "metaphysical
poetry."

When that Queene ended here her progresse time
And, as t'her standing house to heaven did climb,

Here Donne's metaphor takes seriously the doctrine
of the Divinity of Kings. The Ruler is to the body
politic as the soul is to the body. Sickness or departure
of the Ruler is sickness or death to the state. In fact
he is just reversing the metaphor which created the
doctrine of Divine Right. He adds a pun. A Queen
made royal progresses through her dominions so that
her subjects might come together and realize themselves as a State in her. But the soul, as in Bunyan,
also makes a pilgrim's progress. Her "standing
house" is where she *rests* at the end of her progress.
Compare Augustine: "Thou has made us for Thyself
and our souls are restless until they find their rest
in Thee."

Where loath to make the Saints attend her long,
She's now a part both of the Quire, and Song,

A soul so conceived need not delay in joining the company of the Saints. *Quire*: How deep we could take this word you can see from Ruskin's note in *Munera Pulveris*. But the main point of the line is that the Soul becomes both a singer and the song. That goes to the heart of Aristotelianism—where the Divine thinking is one with the object of its thought. (Metaphysics 1075 a). It is itself that thought (or intellect) thinks, on account of its participation in the object of thought: for it becomes its own object in the act of apprehending it: so that thought (intellect) and what is thought of are one and the same. We come back here to our founding questions where the distinction between matter and activity vanishes— as it does for the modern physicist when his ultimate particles become merely what they do.

But to elucidate Donne's line it is better perhaps just to quote another poet: from the last verse of W. B. Yeats's "Among School Children" in *The Tower*:

O Chestnut tree, great rooted blossomer,
Are you the leaf, the blossom or the bole?
O body swayed to music, O brightening glance,
How can we know the dancer from the dance?

or this from T. S. Eliot's *Burnt Norton*:

At the still point of the turning world . . .
    at the still point, there the dance is,
But neither arrest nor movement. And do not call
    it fixity . . .
    Except for the point, the still point,

There would be no dance, and there is only the
dance.

Donne's next line contains the word upon which,
with the word Soule—as on two poles—the entire
interpretation of this poem turns, as for that matter
all philosophy must, the word *world*.

This world, in that great earthquake languished;

world: not of course this planet, the earth, but this
present life as opposed to the other, the realm of de-
parted spirits. Or more narrowly "the pursuits and
interests of the earthly life," as the *Oxford Dictionary* puts it, with the note, "especially in religious use,
the least worthy of these." Donne was extremely fond
of playing with the word "world." It is one of the
chief of his wonder workers. Compare *A Valediction
of Weeping*:

> On a round ball
> A workman that hath copies by, can lay
> An Europe, Afrique, and an Asia,
> And quickly make that which was nothing, *All,*
> So doth each teare,
> Which thee doth weare,
> A globe, yea world by that impression grow,
> Till thy tears mixt with mine doe overflow
> This world, by waters sent from thee, my heaven
> dissolved so.

That is metaphysical metaphor at its height.
Philosophically it is the age-old recognition that, as
Blake put it, "The eye altering, alters all." Donne, of
course, plays throughout his poem on shifts between

the private solipsistic world and the general public world of mundane interests. It is his general theme that both these worlds die, corrupt and disintegrate in the absence of the Soule—as defined in the parenthesis of lines 3 to 6.

Is this extravagance? Is the poem a "preposterous eulogy"? Is it not rather that Donne is saying something which if said in our everyday style would seem so commonplace that we would not notice what we were saying? If so, what was he saying? To put it with our usual crude and unilluminating briefness, he was saying that Elizabeth Drury was an example, an inspiration, and would have been to all who knew her. That looks little enough to say, *if so said*. It took a Donne to expand the implications of those two words "example" and "inspiration" into the poem. But the more we look into the poem, the more we will discover that the understanding of those two words is an understanding of the whole Platonic Aristotelian account of the fabric of things. These words take their meaning, by participation, directly from the founding questions. The best witness will be the closing lines of *The Second Anniversary*:

>   nor would'st thou be content,
> To take this, for my second yeares true Rent,
> Did this Coine beare any other stampe, than his,
> That gave thee power to doe, me, to say this.
> Since his will is, that to posteritie,
> Thou should'st for life, and death, a patterne bee,
> And that the world should notice have of this:

The purpose, and th'authoritie is his;
Thou art the Proclamation; and I am
The Trumpet, at whose voyce the people came.

To read the poem rightly would be to hear and come.

THE NOBLE RIDER AND THE SOUND OF WORDS

OF WORDS

BY WALLACE STEVENS

THE NOBLE RIDER AND THE SOUND
OF WORDS

WALLACE STEVENS

$\mathcal{I}$N THE *Phaedrus,* Plato speaks of the soul in a figure. He says: "Let our figure be of a composite nature—a pair of winged horses and a charioteer. Now the winged horses and the charioteer of the gods are all of them noble, and of noble breed, while ours are mixed; and we have a charioteer who drives them in a pair, and one of them is noble and of noble origin, and the other is ignoble and of ignoble origin; and, as might be expected, there is a great deal of trouble in managing them. I will endeavor to explain to you in what way the mortal differs from the immortal creature. The soul or animate being has the care of the inanimate, and traverses the whole heaven in divers forms appearing;—when perfect and fully winged she soars upward, and is the ruler of the universe; while the imperfect soul loses her feathers, and drooping in her flight at last settles on the solid ground."

We recognize at once, in this figure, Plato's pure poetry; and at the same time we recognize what Coleridge called Plato's dear, gorgeous nonsense. The truth is that we have scarcely read the passage before we have identified ourselves with the charioteer, have, in fact, taken his place and, driving his winged horses, are traversing the whole heaven. Then suddenly we remember, it may be, that the soul no longer exists and we droop in our flight and at last settle on the solid ground. The figure becomes antiquated and rustic.

I

What really happens in this brief experience? Why does this figure, potent for so long, become merely the emblem of a mythology, the rustic memorial of a belief in the soul and in a distinction between good and evil? The answer to these questions is, I think, a simple one.

I said that suddenly we remember that the soul no longer exists and we droop in our flight. For that matter, neither charioteers nor chariots any longer exist. Consequently, the figure does not become unreal because we are troubled about the soul. Besides, unreal things have a reality of their own, in poetry as elsewhere. We do not hesitate, in poetry, to yield ourselves to the unreal, when it is possible to yield ourselves. The existence of the soul, of charioteers and chariots and of winged horses is immaterial. They did not exist for Plato, not even the charioteer and chariot; for certainly a charioteer driving his chariot across the whole heaven was for Plato precisely what he is for us. He was unreal for Plato as he is for us. Plato, however, could yield himself, was free to yield himself, to this gorgeous nonsense. We cannot yield ourselves. We are not free to yield ourselves.

Just as the difficulty is not a difficulty about unreal things, since the imagination accepts them, and since the poetry of the passage is, for us, wholly the poetry of the unreal, so it is not an emotional difficulty. Something else than the imagination is moved by the statement that the horses of the gods are all of them noble, and of noble breed or origin. The statement is a moving statement and is intended to be so. It is insistent and its insistence moves us. Its insistence is the insistence of a speaker, in this case Socrates, who, for the moment, feels delight, even if a casual delight, in the nobility and noble breed. Those images of nobility instantly become nobility itself and determine the emotional level at which the next page or two are to be read. The figure does not lose its vitality because of any failure of feeling on Plato's part. He does not communicate nobility coldly. His horses are not marble horses, the reference to their breed saves them from being that. The fact that the horses are not marble horses helps, moreover, to save the charioteer from being, say, a creature of cloud. The result is that we recognize, even if we cannot realize, the feelings of the robust poet clearly and fluently noting the images in his mind and by means of his robustness, clearness and fluency communicating much more than the images themselves. Yet we do not quite yield. We cannot. We do not feel free.

In trying to find out what it is that stands between Plato's figure and ourselves, we have to accept the idea that, however legendary it appears to be, it has had its vicissitudes. The history of a figure of speech or the history of an idea, such as the idea of nobility, cannot be very different from the history of anything else. It is the episodes that are of interest, and here the episode is that of our diffidence. By us and ourselves, I mean you and me; and yet not you and me as individuals but as representatives of a state of mind. Adams in his work on Vico makes the remark that the true history of the human race is a history of its progressive mental states. It is a remark of interest in this relation. We may assume that in the history of Plato's figure there have been incessant changes of response; that these changes have been psychological changes, and that our own diffidence is simply one more state of mind due to such a change.

The specific question is partly as to the nature of the change and partly as to the cause of it. In nature, the change is as follows: The imagination loses vitality as it ceases to adhere to what is real. When it adheres to the unreal and intensifies what is unreal, while its first effect may be extraordinary, that effect is the maximum effect that it will ever have. In Plato's figure, his imagination does not adhere to what is real. On the contrary, having created something unreal, it adheres to it and intensifies its unreality. Its first effect, its effect at first reading, is its maximum effect, when the imagination, being moved, puts us in the place of the charioteer, before the reason checks us. The case is, then, that we concede that the figure is all imagination. At the same time, we say that it has not the slightest meaning for us, except for its nobility. As to that, while we are moved by it, we are moved as observers. We recognize it perfectly. We do not realize it. We understand the feeling of it, the robust feeling, clearly and fluently communicated. Yet we understand it rather than participate in it.

As to the cause of the change, it is the loss of the figure's vitality. The reason why this particular figure has lost its vitality is that, in it, the imagination adheres to what is unreal. What happened, as we were traversing the whole heaven, is that the imagination lost its power to sustain us. It has the strength of reality or none at all.

II

What has just been said demonstrates that there are degrees of the imagination, as, for example, degrees of vitality and, therefore, of intensity. It is an implication that there are degrees of reality. The discourse about the two elements seems endless. For my own part, I intend merely to follow, in a very hasty way, the fortunes of the idea of nobility as a characteristic of the imagination, and even as its symbol or alter ego, through several of the episodes in its history, in order to determine, if possible, what its fate has been and what has determined its fate. This can be done only on the basis of the relation between the imagination and reality. What has been said in respect to the figure of the charioteer illustrates this.

I should like now to go on to other illustrations of the relation between the imagination and reality and particularly to illustrations that constitute episodes in the history of the idea of nobility. It would be agreeable to pass directly from the charioteer and his winged horses to Don Quixote. It would be like a return from what Plato calls "the back of heaven" to one's own spot. Nevertheless, there is Verrochio (as one among others) with his statue of Bartolommeo Colleoni, in Venice, standing in the way. I have not selected him as a Neo-Platonist to relate us back from a modern time to Plato's time, although he does in fact so relate us, just as through Leonardo, his pupil, he strengthens the relationship. I have selected him because there, on the edge of the world in which we live today, he established a form of such nobility that it has never ceased to magnify us in our own eyes. It is like the form of an invincible man, who has come, slowly and boldly, through every warlike opposition of the past and who moves in our midst without dropping the bridle of the powerful horse from his hand, without taking off his helmet and without relaxing the attitude of a warrior of noble origin. What man on whose side the horseman fought could ever be anything but fearless, anything but indomitable? One feels the passion of rhetoric begin to stir and even to grow furious; and one thinks that, after all, the noble style, in whatever it creates, merely perpetuates the noble style. In this statue, the apposition between the imagination and reality is too favorable to the imagination. Our difficulty is not primarily with any detail. It is primarily with the whole. The point is not so much to analyze the difficulty as to determine whether we share it, to find out whether it exists, whether we regard this specimen of the genius of Verrochio and of the Renaissance as a bit of uncommon panache, no longer quite the appropriate thing outdoors, or whether we regard it, in the language of Dr. Richards, as something inexhaustible to meditation or, to speak for myself, as a thing of a nobility responsive to the most minute demand. It seems, nowadays, what it may very well not have seemed a few years ago, a little overpowering, a little magnificent.

Undoubtedly, Don Quixote could be Bartolommeo Colleoni in Spain. The tradition of Italy is the tradition of the imagination. The tradition of Spain is the tradition of reality. There is no apparent reason why the reverse should not be true. If this is a just observation, it indicates that the relation between the imagination and reality is a question, more or less, of precise equilibrium. Thus it is not a question of the difference between grotesque extremes. My purpose is not to contrast Colleoni with Don Quixote. It is to say that one passed into the other, that one became, and was, the other. The difference between them is that Verrochio believed in one kind of nobility and Cervantes, if he believed in any, believed in another kind. With Verrochio it was an affair of the noble style, whatever his prepossession respecting the nobility of man as a real animal may have been. With Cervantes, nobility was not a thing of the imagination. It was a part of reality, it was something that exists in life, something so true to us that it is in danger of ceasing to exist, if we isolate it, something in the mind of a precarious tenure. These may be words. Certainly, however, Cervantes sought to set right the balance between the imagination and reality. As we come closer to our own times in Don Quixote and as we are drawn together by the intelligence common to the two periods, we may derive so much satisfaction from the restoration of reality as to become wholly prejudiced against the imagination. This is to reach a conclusion prematurely, let alone that it may be to reach a conclusion in respect to something as to which no conclusion is possible or desirable.

There is in Washington, in Lafayette Square, which is the square on which the White House faces, a statue of Andrew Jackson, riding a horse with one of the most beautiful tails in the world. General Jackson is raising his hat in a gay gesture, saluting the ladies of his generation. One looks at this work of Clark Mills and thinks of the remark of Bertrand Russell that to acquire immunity to eloquence is of the utmost importance to the citizens of a democracy. We are bound to think that Colleoni, as a mercenary, was a much less formidable man than General Jackson, that he meant less to fewer people and that, if Verrochio could have applied his prodigious poetry to Jackson, the whole American outlook today might be imperial. This work is a work of fancy. Dr. Richards cites Coleridge's theory of fancy as opposed to imagination. Fancy is an activity of the mind which puts things together of choice, *not* the will, as a principle of the mind's being, striving to realize itself in knowing itself. Fancy, then, is an exercise of selection from among objects already supplied by association, a selection made for purposes which are not then and therein being shaped but have been already fixed. We are concerned then with an object occupying a position as remarkable as any that can be found in the United States in which there is not the slightest trace of the imagination. Treating this work as typical, it is obvious that the American will as a principle of the mind's being is easily satisfied in its efforts to realize itself in knowing itself. The statue may be dismissed, not without speaking of it again as a thing that at least makes us conscious of ourselves as we were, if not as we are. To that extent, it helps us to know ourselves. It helps us to know ourselves as we were and that helps us to know ourselves as we are. The statue is neither of the imagination nor of reality. That it is a work of fancy precludes it from being a work of the imagination. A glance at it shows it to be unreal. The bearing of this is that there can be works, and this includes poems, in which neither the imagination nor reality is present.

The other day I was reading a note about an American artist who was said to have "turned his back on the esthetic whims and theories of the day, and established headquarters in lower Manhattan." Accompanying this note was a reproduction of a painting called "Wooden Horses." It is a painting of a merry-go-round, possibly of several of them. One of the horses seems to be prancing. The others are going lickety-split, each one struggling to get the bit in his teeth. The horse in the center of the picture, painted yellow, has two riders, one a man, dressed in a carnival costume, who is seated in the saddle, the other a blonde, who is seated well up the horse's neck. The man has his arms under the girl's arms. He holds himself stiffly in order to keep his cigar out of the girl's hair. Her feet are in a second and shorter set of stirrups. She has the legs of a hammer-thrower. It is clear that the couple are accustomed to wooden horses and like them. A little behind them is a younger girl riding alone. She has a strong body and streaming hair. She wears a short-sleeved, red waist, a white skirt and an emphatic bracelet of pink coral. She has her eyes on the man's arms. Still farther behind, there is another girl. One does not see much more of her than her head. Her lips are painted bright red. It seems that it would be better if some one were to hold her on her horse. We, here, are not interested in any aspect of this picture except that it is a picture of ribald and hilarious reality. It is a picture wholly favorable to what is real. It is not without imagination and it is far from being without esthetic theory.

III

These illustrations of the relation between the imagination and reality are an outline on the basis of which to indicate a tendency. Their usefulness is this: that they help to make clear, what no one may ever have doubted, that just as in this or that work the degrees of the imagination and of reality may vary, so this variation may exist as between the works of one age and the works of another. What I have said up to this point amounts to this: that the idea of nobility exists in art today only in degenerate forms or in a much diminished state, if, in fact, it exists at all or otherwise than on sufferance; that this is due to failure in the relation between the imagination and reality. I should now like to add that this failure is due, in turn, to the pressure of reality.

A variation between the sound of words in one age and the sound of words in another age is an instance of the pressure of reality. Take the statement by Bateson that a language, considered semantically, evolves through a series of conflicts between the denotative and the connotative forces in words; between an asceticism tending to kill language by stripping words of all association and a hedonism tending to kill language by dissipating their sense in a multiplicity of associations. These conflicts are nothing more than changes in the relation between the imagination and reality. Bateson describes the seventeenth century in England as predominately a connotative period. The use of words in connotative senses was denounced by Locke and Hobbes, who desired a mathematical plainness, in short, perspicuous words. There followed in the eighteenth century an era of poetic diction. This was not the language of the age but a language of poetry peculiar to itself. In time, Wordsworth came to write the preface to the second edition of the *Lyrical Ballads* (1800) in which he said that the first volume had been published, "as an experiment, which, I hoped, might be of some use to ascertain how far, by fitting to metrical arrangement a selection of the real language of man in a state of vivid sensation, that sort of pleasure and that quantity of pleasure may be imparted, which a Poet may rationally endeavor to impart."

As the nineteenth century progressed, language once more became connotative. While there have been intermediate reactions, this tendency toward the connotative is the tendency today. The interest in semantics is evidence of this. In the case of some of our prose writers, as, for example, Joyce, the language, in quite different ways, is wholly connotative. When we say that Locke and Hobbes denounced the connotative use of words as an abuse, and when we speak of reactions and reforms, we are speaking, on the one hand, of a failure of the imagination to adhere to reality, and, on the other, of a use of language favorable to reality. The statement that the tendency toward the connotative is the tendency today is disputable. The general movement in the arts, that is to say, in painting and in music, has been the other way. It is hard to say that the tendency is toward the connotative in the use of words without also saying that the tendency is toward the imagination in other directions. The interest in the subconscious and in surrealism shows the tendency toward the imaginative. Boileau's remark that Descartes had cut poetry's throat is a remark that could have been made respecting a great many people during the last hundred years, and of no one more aptly than of Freud, who, as it happens, was familiar with it and repeats it in his *Future of an Illusion*. The object of that essay was to suggest a surrender to reality. His premise was that it is the unmistakable character of the present situation not that the promises of religion have become smaller but that they appear less credible to people. He notes the decline of religious belief and disagrees with the argument that man cannot in general do without the consolation of what he calls the religious illusion and that without it he would not endure the cruelty of reality. His conclusion is that man must venture at last into the hostile world and that this may be called education to reality. There is much more in that essay inimical to poetry and not least the observation in one of the final pages that, "The voice of the intellect is a soft one, but it does not rest until it has gained a hearing." This, I fear, is intended to be the voice of the realist.

A tendency in language toward the connotative might very well parallel a tendency in other arts toward the denotative. We have just seen that that is in fact the situation. I suppose that the present always appears to be an illogical complication. The language of Joyce goes along with the dilapidations of Braque and Picasso and the music of the Austrians. To the extent that this painting and this music are the work of men who regard it as part of the science of painting and the science of music it is the work of realists. Actually its effect is that of the imagination, just as the effect of abstract painting is so often that of the imagination, although that may be different. Busoni said, in a letter to his wife, "I have made the painful discovery that nobody loves and feels music." Very likely, the reason there is a tendency in language toward the connotative today is that there are many who love it and feel it. It may be that Braque and Picasso love and feel painting and that Schönberg loves and feels music, although it seems that what they love and feel is something else.

A tendency toward the connotative, whether in language or elsewhere, cannot continue against the pressure of reality. If it is the pressure of reality that controls poetry, then the immediacy of various theories of poetry is not what it was. For instance, when Rostrevor Hamilton says, "The object of contemplation is the highly complex and unified content of consciousness, which comes into being through the developing subjective attitude of the percipient," he has in mind no such "content of consciousness" as every newspaper reader experiences today.

By way of further illustration, let me quote from Croce's Oxford lecture of 1933. He said: "If . . . poetry is intuition and expression, the fusion of sound and imagery, what is the material which takes on the form of sound and imagery? It is the whole man: the man who thinks and wills, and loves, and hates; who is strong and weak, sublime and pathetic, good and wicked; man in the exultation and agony of living; and together with the man, integral with him, it is all nature in its perpetual labour of evolution. . . . Poetry . . . is the triumph of contemplation . . . Poetic genius chooses a strait path in which passion is calmed and calm is passionate."

Croce cannot have been thinking of a world in which all normal life is at least in suspense, or, if you like, under blockade. He was thinking of normal human experience.

Quite apart from the abnormal aspect of everyday life today, there is the normal aspect of it. The spirit of negation has been so active, so confident and so intolerant that the commonplaces about the romantic provoke us to wonder if our salvation, if the way out, is not the romantic. All the great things have been denied and we live in an intricacy of new and local mythologies, political, economic, poetic, which are asserted with an ever-enlarging incoherence. This is accompanied by an absence of any authority except force, operative or imminent. What has been called the disparagement of reason is an instance of the absence of authority. We pick up the radio and find that comedians regard the public use of words of more than two syllables as funny. We read of the opening of the National Gallery at Washington and we are convinced, in the end, that the pictures are counterfeit, that museums are impositions and that Mr. Mellon was a monster. We turn to a recent translation of Kierkegaard and we find him saying: "A great deal has been said about poetry reconciling one with existence; rather it might be said that it arouses one against existence; for poetry is unjust to men . . . it has use only for the elect, but that is a poor sort of reconciliation. I will take the case of sickness. Esthetics replies proudly and quite consistently, 'That cannot be employed, poetry must not become a hospital.' Esthetics culminates . . . by regarding sickness in accordance with the principle enunciated by Friederick Schlegel: 'Nur Gesundheit ist liebenswurdig.' (Health alone is lovable.)"

The enormous influence of education in giving everyone a little learning, and in giving large groups considerably more: something of history, something of philosophy, something of literature; the expansion of the middle class with its common preference for realistic satisfactions; the penetration of the masses of people by the ideas of liberal thinkers, even when that penetration is indirect, as by the reporting of the reasons why people oppose the ideas that they oppose, —these are normal aspects of everyday life. The way we live and the way we work alike cast us out on reality. If fifty private houses were to be built in New York this year, it would be a phenomenon. We no longer live in homes but in housing projects and this is so whether the project is literally a project or a club, a dormitory, a camp or an apartment in River House. It is not only that there are more of us and that we are actually close together. We are close together in every way. We lie in bed and listen to a broadcast from Cairo, and so on. There is no distance. We are intimate with people we have never seen and, unhappily, they are intimate with us. Democritus plucked his eye out because he could not look at a woman without thinking of her as a woman. If he had read a few of our novels, he would have torn himself to pieces. Dr. Richards has noted, "the widespread increase in the aptitude of the average mind for self-dissolving introspection, the generally heightened awareness of the goings-on of our own minds, *merely as goings-on.*" This is nothing to the generally heightened awareness of the goings-on of other people's minds, *merely as goings-on.* The way we work is a good deal more difficult for the imagination than the highly civilized revolution that is occurring in respect to work indicates. It is, in the main, a revolution for more pay. We have been assured, by every visitor, that the American businessman is absorbed in his business and there is nothing to be gained by disputing it. As for the workers, it is enough to say that the word has grown to be literary. They have become, at their work, in the face of the machines, something approximating an abstraction, an energy. The time must be coming when, as they leave the factories, they will be passed through an air-chamber or a bar to revive them for riot and reading. I am sorry to have to add that to one that thinks, as Dr. Richards thinks, that poetry is the supreme use of language, some of the foreign universities in relation to our own, appear to be, so far as the things of the imagination are concerned, as Verrocchio is to the sculptor of the statue of General Jackson.

These, nevertheless, are not the things that I had in mind when I spoke of the pressure of reality. These constitute the drift of incidents, to which we accustom ourselves as to the weather. Materialism is an old story and an indifferent one. Robert Wolseley said: "True genius . . . will enter into the hardest and dryest thing, enrich the most barren Soyl, and inform the meanest and most uncomely matter . . . the baser, the emptier, the obscurer, the fouler, and the less susceptible of Ornament the subject appears to be, the more is the Poet's Praise . . . who, as Horace says of Homer, can fetch Light out of Smoak, Roses out of Dunghills, and give a kind of Life to the Inanimate . . ." (Preface to Rochester's

Valentinian, 1685, Eng. Assoc. St. 1939). By the
pressure of reality, I mean the pressure of an external event or events on the consciousness to the
exclusion of any power of contemplation. The definition ought to be exact and, as it is, may be merely
pretentious. But when one is trying to think of a
whole generation and of a world at war, and trying
at the same time to see what is happening to the
imagination, particularly if one believes that that
is what matters most, the plainest statement of what
is happening can easily appear to be an affectation.

For more than ten years now, there has been an
extraordinary pressure of news, let us say, news in-
comparably more pretentious than any description
of it, news, at first, of the collapse of our system, or,
call it, of life; then of news of a new world, but of a
new world so uncertain that one did not know anything whatever of its nature, and does not know now,
and could not tell whether it was to be all-English,
all-German, all-Russian, all-Japanese, or all-Amer-
ican, and cannot tell now; and finally news of a war,
which was a renewal of what, if it was not the greatest war, became such by this continuation. And for
more than ten years, the consciousness of the world
has concentrated on events which have made the
ordinary movement of life seem to be the movement
of people in the intervals of a storm. The disclosures
of the impermanence of the past suggested, and suggest, an impermanence of the future. Little of what
we have believed has been true. Only the prophecies

are true. The present is an opportunity to repent. This is familiar enough. The war is only a part of a war-like whole. It is not possible to look backward and to see that the same thing was true in the past. It is a question of pressure, and pressure is incalculable and eludes the historian. The Napoleonic era is regarded as having had little or no effect on the poets and the novelists who lived in it. But Coleridge and Wordsworth and Sir Walter Scott and Jane Austen did not have to put up with Napoleon and Marx and Europe, Asia and Africa all at one time. It seems possible to say that they knew of the events of their day much as we know of the bombings in the interior of China and not at all as we know of the bombings of London, or, rather, as we should know of the bombings of Toronto or Montreal. Another part of the war-like whole to which we do not respond quite as we do to the news of war is the income tax. The blanks are specimens of mathematical prose. They titillate the instinct of self-preservation in a class in which that instinct has been forgotten. Virginia Woolf thought that the income tax, if it continued, would benefit poets by enlarging their vocabularies and I dare say that she was right.

If it is not possible to assert that the Napoleonic era was the end of one era in the history of the imagination and the beginning of another, one comes closer to the truth by making that assertion in respect to the French Revolution. The defeat or triumph of

Hitler are parts of a war-like whole but the fate of
an individual is different from the fate of a society.
Rightly or wrongly, we feel that the fate of a society
is involved in the orderly disorders of the present
time. We are confronting, therefore, a set of events,
not only beyond our power to tranquillize them in
the mind, beyond our power to reduce them and meta-
morphose them, but events that stir the emotions to
violence, that engage us in what is direct and immediate and real, and events that involve the concepts
and sanctions that are the order of our lives and may
involve our very lives; and these events are occurring
persistently, with increasing omen, in what may be
called our presence. These are the things that I had
in mind when I spoke of the pressure of reality, a
pressure great enough and prolonged enough to bring
about the end of one era in the history of the imagination and, if so, then great enough to bring about
the beginning of another. It is one of the peculiarities
of the imagination that it is always at the end of
an era. What happens is that it is always attaching
itself to a new reality, and adhering to it. It is not
that there is a new imagination but that there is a
new reality. The pressure of reality may, of course,
be less than the general pressure that I have described.
It exists for individuals according to the circumstances of their lives or according to the characteristics of their minds. To sum it up, the pressure of
reality is, I think, the determining factor in the
artistic character of an era and, as well, the determin-

ing factor in the artistic character of an individual. The resistance to this pressure or its evasion in the case of individuals of extraordinary imagination cancels the pressure so far as those individuals are concerned.

IV

Suppose we try, now, to construct the figure of a poet, a possible poet. He cannot be a charioteer traversing vacant space, however ethereal. He must have lived all of the last two thousand years, and longer, and he must have instructed himself, as best he could, as he went along. He will have thought that Virgil, Dante, Shakespeare, Milton placed themselves in remote lands and in remote ages; that their men and women were the dead—and not the dead lying in the earth, but the dead still living in their remote lands and in their remote ages, and living in the earth or under it, or in the heavens—and he will wonder at those huge imaginations, in which what is remote becomes near, and what is dead lives with an intensity beyond any experience of life. He will consider that although he has himself witnessed, during the long period of his life, a general transition to reality, his own measure as a poet, in spite of all the passions of all the lovers of the truth, is the measure of his power to abstract himself, and to withdraw with him into his abstraction, the reality on which the lovers of truth insist. He must be able to abstract himself and also to abstract reality, which he does by placing it in his imagination. He knows perfectly that he cannot be too noble a rider, that he cannot rise up loftily in helmet and armor on a horse of imposing bronze. He will think again of Milton and of what was said about him: that "the necessity of writing for one's living blunts the appreciation of writing when it bears the mark of perfection. Its quality disconcerts our hasty writers; they are ready to condemn it as preciosity and affectation. And if to them the musical and creative powers of words convey little pleasure, how out of date and irrelevant they must find the . . . music of Milton's verse." Don Quixote will make it imperative for him to make a choice, to come to a decision regarding the imagination and reality; and he will find that it is not a choice of one over the other and not a decision that divides them, but something subtler, a recognition that here, too, as between these poles, the universal interdependence exists, and hence his choice and his decision must be that they are equal and inseparable. To take a single instance: When Horatio says,

> Now cracks a noble heart. Good night, sweet prince,
> And flights of angels sing thee to thy rest!

are not the imagination and reality equal and inseparable? Above all, he will not forget General Jackson or the picture of the "Wooden Horses."

I said of the picture that it was a work in which everything was favorable to reality. I hope that the use of that bare word has been enough. But without regard to its range of meaning in thought, it includes all its natural images and its connotations are without limit. Bergson describes the visual perception of a motionless object as the most stable of internal states. He says, "The object may remain the same, I may look at it from the same side, at the same angle, in the same light; nevertheless, the vision I now have of it differs from that which I have just had, even if only because the one is an instant later than the other. My memory is there, which conveys something of the past into the present."

Dr. Joad's comment on this is, "Similarly with external things. Every body, every quality of a body resolves itself into an enormous number of vibrations, movements, changes. What is it that vibrates, moves, is changed? There is no answer. Philosophy has long dismissed the notion of substance and modern physics has endorsed the dismissal. . . . How, then, does the world come to appear to us as a collection of solid, static objects extended in space? Because of the intellect, which presents us with a false view of it."

The poet has his own meaning for reality, and the painter has, and the musician has; and besides what it means to the intelligence and to the senses, it means something to everyone, so to speak. Notwithstanding this, the word in its general sense, which is the sense in which I have used it, adapts itself instantly. The subject-matter of poetry is not that "collection of solid, static objects extended in space" but the life that is lived in the scene that it composes; and so reality is not that external scene but the life that is lived in it. Reality is things as they are. The general sense of the word proliferates its special senses. It is a jungle in itself. As in the case of a jungle, everything that makes it up is pretty much of one color. First, then, there is the reality that is taken for granted, that is latent and, on the whole, ignored. It is the comfortable American state of life of the 'eighties, the 'nineties and the first ten years of the present century. Next, there is the reality that has ceased to be indifferent, the years when the Victorians had been disposed of and intellectual minorities and social minorities began to take their place and to convert our state of life to something that might not be final. This much more vital reality made the life that had preceded it look like a volume of Ackermann's colored plates or one of Töpfer's books of sketches in Switzerland. I am trying to give the feel of it. It was the reality of twenty or thirty years ago. I say that it was a vital reality. The phrase gives a false impression. It was vital in the sense of being tense, of being instinct with the fatal or with what might be the fatal. The minorities began to convince us that the Victorians had left nothing behind. The Russians followed the Victorians and the Germans, in their way, followed the Russians. The British Empire, directly or indirectly, was what was left and as to that one could not be sure whether it was a shield or a target. Reality then became violent and so remains. This much ought to be said to make it a little clearer that in speaking of the pressure of reality, I am thinking of life in a state of violence, not physically violent, as yet, for us in America, but physically violent for millions of our friends and for still more millions of our enemies and spiritually violent, it may be said, for everyone alive.

A possible poet must be a poet capable of resisting or evading the pressure of the reality of this last degree, with the knowledge that the degree of today may become a deadlier degree tomorrow. There is, however, no point to dramatizing the future in advance of the fact. I confine myself to the outline of a possible poet, with only the slightest sketch of his background.

v

Here I am, well-advanced in my paper, with everything of interest that I started out to say remaining to be said. I am interested in the nature of poetry and I have stated its nature, from one of the many points of view from which it is possible to state it. It is an interdependence of the imagination and reality as equals. This is not a definition, since it is incomplete. But it states the nature of poetry. Then I am interested in the rôle of the poet and this is paramount. In this area of my subject I might be expected to speak of the social, that is to say sociological or political, obligation of the poet. He has none. That he must be contemporaneous is as old as Longinus and I dare say older. But that he *is* contemporaneous is almost inevitable. How contemporaneous in the direct sense in which being contemporaneous is intended were the four great poets of whom I spoke a moment ago? I do not think that a poet owes any more as a social obligation than he owes as a moral obligation, and if there is anything concerning poetry about which people agree it is that the rôle of the poet is not to be found in morals. I cannot say what that wide agreement amounts to because the agreement (in which I do not join) that the poet is under a social obligation is equally wide. Reality is life and life is society and the imagination and reality, that is to say, the imagination and society are inseparable. That is preeminently true in the case of the poetic drama. The poetic drama needs a terrible genius before it is anything more than a literary relic. Besides the theater has forgotten that it could ever be terrible. It is not one of the instruments of fate, decidedly. Yes: the all-commanding subject-matter of poetry is life, the never-ceasing source. But it is not a social obligation. One does not love and go back to one's ancient mother as a social obligation. One goes back out of a suasion not to be denied. Unquestionably if a social movement moved one deeply enough, its moving poems would follow. No politician can command the imagination, directing it to do this or that. Stalin might grind his teeth the whole of a Russian winter and yet all the poets in the Soviets might remain silent the following spring. He might excite their imaginations by something he said or did. He would not command them.

He is singularly free from that "cult of pomp," which is the comic side of the European disaster; and that means as much as anything to us. The truth is that the social obligation so closely urged is a phase of the pressure of reality which a poet (in the absence of dramatic poets) is bound to resist or evade today. Dante in Purgatory and Paradise was still the voice of the Middle Ages but not through fulfilling any social obligation. Since that is the rôle most frequently urged, if that rôle is eliminated, and if a possible poet is left facing life without any categorical exactions upon him, what then? What is his function? Certainly it is not to lead people out of the confusion in which they find themselves. Nor is it, I think, to comfort them while they follow their leaders to and fro. I think that his function is to make his imagination theirs and that he fulfils himself only as he sees his imagination become the light in the minds of others. His rôle, in short, is to help people to live their lives. Time and time again it has been said that he may not address himself to an élite. I think he may. There is not a poet whom we prize living today that does not address himself to an élite. The poet will continue to do this: to address himself to an élite even in a classless society, unless, perhaps, this exposes him to imprisonment or exile. In that event he is likely not to address himself to anyone at all. He may, like Shostakovitch, content himself with pretence. He will, nevertheless, still be addressing himself to an élite, for all poets address themselves to someone and it is of the essence of that instinct, and it seems to amount to an instinct, that it should be to an élite, not to a drab but to a woman with the hair of a pythoness, not to a chamber of commerce but to a gallery of one's own, if there are enough of one's own to fill a gallery. And that élite, if it responds, not out of complaisance, but because the poet has quickened it, because he has educed from it that for which it was searching in itself and in the life around it and which it had not yet quite found, will thereafter do for the poet what he cannot do for himself, that is to say: receive his poetry.

I repeat that his rôle is to help people to live their lives. He has had immensely to do with giving life whatever savor it possesses. He has had to do with whatever the imagination and the senses have made of the world. He has, in fact, had to do with life except as the intellect has had to do with it and, as to that, no one is needed to tell us that poetry and philosophy are akin. I want to repeat for two reasons a number of observations made by Charles Mauron. The first reason is that these observations tell us what it is that a poet does to help people to live their lives and the second is that they prepare the way for a word concerning escapism. They are: that the artist transforms us into epicures; that he has to discover the possible work of art in the real world, then to extract it, when he does not himself compose it entirely; that he is *un amoureux perpétuel* of the world that he contemplates and thereby enriches; that art sets out to express the human soul; and finally that everything like a firm grasp of reality is eliminated from the esthetic field. With these aphorisms in mind, how is it possible to condemn escapism? The poetic process is psychologically an escapist process. The chatter about escapism is, to my way of thinking, merely common cant. My own remarks about resisting or evading the pressure of reality mean escapism, if analyzed. Escapism has a pejorative sense, which it cannot be supposed that I include in the sense in which I use the word. The pejorative sense applies where the poet is not attached to reality, where the imagination does not adhere to reality, which, for my part, I regard as fundamental. If we go back to the collection of solid, static objects extended in space, which Dr. Joad posited, and if we say that the space is blank space, nowhere, without color, and that the objects, though solid, have no shadows and, though static, exert a mournful power, and, without elaborating this complete poverty, if suddenly we hear a different and familiar description of the place:

> This City now doth, like a garment, wear
> The beauty of the morning; silent, bare,
> Ships, towers, domes, theatres, and temples lie
> Open unto the fields, and to the sky;
> All bright and glittering in the smokeless air;

if we have this experience, we know how poets help people to live their lives. This illustration must serve for all the rest. There is, in fact, a world of poetry indistinguishable from the world in which we live, or, I ought to say, no doubt, from the world in which we shall come to live, since what makes the poet the potent figure that he is, or was, or ought to be, is that he creates the world to which we turn incessantly and without knowing it and that he gives to life the supreme fictions without which we are unable to conceive of it.

And what about the sound of words? What about nobility, of which the fortunes were to be a kind of test of the value of the poet? I do not know of anything that will appear to have suffered more from the passage of time than the music of poetry and that has suffered less. The deepening need for words to express our thoughts and feelings which, we are sure, are all the truth that we shall ever experience, having no illusions, makes us listen to words when we hear them, loving them and feeling them, makes us search the sound of them, for a finality, a perfection, an unalterable vibration, which it is only within the power of the acutest poet to give them. Those of us who may have been thinking of the path of poetry, those who understand that words are thoughts and not only our own thoughts but the thoughts of men and women ignorant of what it is that they are thinking, must be conscious of this: that, above everything else, poetry is words; and that words, above everything else, are, in poetry, sounds. This being so, my time and yours might have been better spent if I had been less interested in trying to give our possible poet an identity and less interested in trying to appoint him to his place. But unless I had done these things, it might have been thought that I was rhetorical, when I was speaking in the simplest way about things of such importance that nothing is more so. A poet's words are of things that do not exist without the words. Thus, the image of the charioteer and of the winged horses, which has been held to be precious for all of time that matters, was created by words of things that never existed without the words. A description of Verrocchio's statue could be the integration of an illusion equal to the statue itself. Poetry is a revelation in words by means of the words. Croce was not speaking of poetry in particular when he said that language is perpetual creation. About nobility, I cannot be sure that the decline, not to say the disappearance of nobility is anything more than a maladjustment between the imagination and reality. We have been a little insane about the truth. We have had an obsession. In its ultimate extension, the truth about which we have been insane will lead us to look beyond the truth to something in which the imagination will be the dominant complement. It is not only that the imagination adheres to reality, but, also, that reality adheres to the imagination and that the interdependence is essential. We may emerge from our *bassesse* and, if we do, how would it happen if not by the intervention of some fortune of the mind? And what would that fortune of the mind happen to be? It might be only commonsense but even that, a commonsense beyond the truth, would be a nobility of long descent.

The poet refuses to allow his task to be set for him. He denies that he has a task and considers that the organization of materia poetica is a contradiction in terms. Yet the imagination gives to everything that it touches a peculiarity, and it seems to me that the peculiarity of the imagination is nobility, of which there are many degrees. This inherent nobility is the natural source of another, which our extremely headstrong generation regards as false and decadent. I mean that nobility which is our spiritual height and depth; and while I know how difficult it is to express it, nevertheless I am bound to give a sense of it. Nothing could be more evasive and inaccessible. Nothing distorts itself and seeks disguise more quickly. There is a shame of disclosing it and in its definite presentations a horror of it. But there it is. The fact that it is there is what makes it possible to invite to the reading and writing of poetry men of intelligence and desire for life. I am not thinking of the ethical or the sonorous or at all of the manner of it. The manner of it is, in fact, its difficulty, which each man must feel each day differently, for himself. I am not thinking of the solemn, the portentous or demoded. On the other hand, I am evading a definition. If it is defined, it will be fixed and it must not be fixed. As in the case of an external thing, nobility resolves itself into an enormous number of vibrations, movements, changes. To fix it is to put an end to it. Let me show it to you unfixed.

Late last year Epstein exhibited some of his flower paintings at The Leicester Galleries in London. A commentator in *Apollo* said, *"How with this rage can beauty hold a plea* . . . The quotation from Shakespeare's 65th sonnet prefaces the catalogue . . . It would be apropos to any other flower paintings than Mr. Epstein's. His make no pretence to fragility. They shout, explode all over the picture space and generally oppose the rage of the world with such a rage of form and colour as no flower in nature or pigment has done since Van Gogh."

What ferocious beauty the line from Shakespeare puts on when used under such circumstances! While it has its modulation of despair, it holds its plea and its plea is noble. There is no element more conspicuously absent from contemporary poetry than nobility. There is no element that poets have sought after, more curiously and more piously, certain of its obscure existence. Its voice is one of the inarticulate voices which it is their business to overhear and to record. The nobility of rhetoric is, of course, a lifeless nobility. Pareto's epigram that history is a cemetery of aristocracies easily becomes another: that poetry is a cemetery of nobilities. For the sensitive poet, conscious of negations, nothing is more difficult than the affirmations of nobility and yet there is nothing that he requires of himself more persistently, since in them and in their kind, alone, are to be found those sanctions that are the reasons for his being and for that occasional ecstasy, or ecstatic freedom of the mind, which is his special privilege.

It is hard to think of a thing more out of time than nobility. Looked at plainly it seems false and dead and ugly. To look at it at all makes us realize sharply that in our present, in the presence of our reality, the past looks false and is, therefore, dead and is, therefore, ugly; and we turn away from it as from something repulsive and particularly from the characteristic that it has a way of assuming: something that was noble in its day, grandeur that was, the rhetorical once. But as a wave is a force and not the water of which it is composed, which is never the same, so nobility is a force and not the manifestations of which it is composed, which are never the same. Possibly this description of it as a force will do more than anything else I can have said about it to reconcile you to it. It is not an artifice that the mind has added to human nature. The mind has added nothing to human nature. It is a violence from within that protects us from a violence without. It is the imagination pressing back against the pressure of reality. It seems, in the last analysis, to have something to do with our self-preservation; and that, no doubt, is why the expression of it, the sound of its words, helps us to live our lives.